INTRODUCING
ISSUES WITH
OPPOSING
VIEWPOINTS®

Intersectionality and Identity Politics

M. M. Eboch, Book Editor

GREENHAVEN
PUBLISHING

Published in 2019 by Greenhaven Publishing, LLC
353 3rd Avenue, Suite 255, New York, NY 10010

Articles in Greenhaven Publishing anthologies are often edited for length to meet page requirements. In addition, original titles of
these works are changed to clearly present the main thesis and to explicitly indicate the author's opinion. Every effort is made to
ensure that Greenhaven Publishing accurately reflects the original intent of the authors. Every effort has been made to trace the
owners of the copyrighted material.

Library of Congress Cataloging-in-Publication Data

Names: Eboch, M. M., editor.
Title: Intersectionality and identity politics / M.M. Eboch, book editor.
Description: New York : Greenhaven Publishing, [2019] | Series: Introducing
  issues with opposing viewpoints | Audience: Grades 7-12. | Includes
  bibliographical references and index.
Identifiers: LCCN 2018023075| ISBN 9781534504240 (library bound) | ISBN
  9781534504851 (pbk.)
Subjects: LCSH: Intersectionality (Sociology)--United States. | Identity
  politics--United States.
Classification: LCC HM488.5 .I584 2019 | DDC 320.0973--dc23
LC record available at https://lccn.loc.gov/2018023075

Manufactured in the United States of America

Website: http://greenhavenpublishing.com

Contents

Foreword

Indulging in a wide spectrum of ideas, beliefs, and perspectives is a critical cornerstone of democracy. After all, it is often debates over differences of opinion, such as whether to legalize abortion, how to treat prisoners, or when to enact the death penalty, that shape our society and drive it forward. Such diversity of thought is frequently regarded as the hallmark of a healthy and civilized culture. As the Reverend Clifford Schutjer of the First Congregational Church in Mansfield, Ohio, declared in a 2001 sermon, "Surrounding oneself with only like-minded people, restricting what we listen to or read only to what we find agreeable is irresponsible. Refusing to entertain doubts once we make up our minds is a subtle but deadly form of arrogance." With this advice in mind, Introducing Issues with Opposing Viewpoints books aim to open readers' minds to the critically divergent views that comprise our world's most important debates.

Introducing Issues with Opposing Viewpoints simplifies for students the enormous and often overwhelming mass of material now available via print and electronic media. Collected in every volume is an array of opinions that captures the essence of a particular controversy or topic. Introducing Issues with Opposing Viewpoints books embody the spirit of nineteenth-century journalist Charles A. Dana's axiom: "Fight for your opinions, but do not believe that they contain the whole truth, or the only truth." Absorbing such contrasting opinions teaches students to analyze the strength of an argument and compare it to its opposition. From this process readers can inform and strengthen their own opinions, or be exposed to new information that will change their minds. Introducing Issues with Opposing Viewpoints is a mosaic of different voices. The authors are statesmen, pundits, academics, journalists, corporations, and ordinary people who have felt compelled to share their experiences and ideas in a public forum. Their words have been collected from newspapers, journals, books, speeches, interviews, and the Internet, the fastest growing body of opinionated material in the world.

Introducing Issues with Opposing Viewpoints shares many of the well-known features of its critically acclaimed parent series, Opposing

Viewpoints. The articles allow readers to absorb and compare divergent perspectives. Active reading questions preface each viewpoint, requiring the student to approach the material thoughtfully and carefully. Photographs, charts, and graphs supplement each article. A thorough introduction provides readers with crucial background on an issue. An annotated bibliography points the reader toward articles, books, and websites that contain additional information on the topic. An appendix of organizations to contact contains a wide variety of charities, nonprofit organizations, political groups, and private enterprises that each hold a position on the issue at hand. Finally, a comprehensive index allows readers to locate content quickly and efficiently.

Introducing Issues with Opposing Viewpoints is also significantly different from Opposing Viewpoints. As the series title implies, its presentation will help introduce students to the concept of opposing viewpoints and learn to use this material to aid in critical writing and debate. The series' four-color, accessible format makes the books attractive and inviting to readers of all levels. In addition, each viewpoint has been carefully edited to maximize a reader's understanding of the content. Short but thorough viewpoints capture the essence of an argument. A substantial, thought-provoking essay question placed at the end of each viewpoint asks the student to further investigate the issues raised in the viewpoint, compare and contrast two authors' arguments, or consider how one might go about forming an opinion on the topic at hand. Each viewpoint contains sidebars that include at-a-glance information and handy statistics. A Facts About section located in the back of the book further supplies students with relevant facts and figures.

Following in the tradition of the Opposing Viewpoints series, Greenhaven Publishing continues to provide readers with invaluable exposure to the controversial issues that shape our world. As John Stuart Mill once wrote: "The only way in which a human being can make some approach to knowing the whole of a subject is by hearing what can be said about it by persons of every variety of opinion and studying all modes in which it can be looked at by every character of mind. No wise man ever acquired his wisdom in any mode but this." It is to this principle that Introducing Issues with Opposing Viewpoints books are dedicated.

Introduction

"[P]eople can suffer real damage ... if the people or society around them mirror back to them a confining or demeaning or contemptible picture of themselves ... Recognition is not just a courtesy we owe people. It is a vital human need."
—*Charles Taylor,* Multicultrualism and "The Politics of Recognition"

America is a land of freedom and opportunity. Everyone is equal. Every adult citizen has an equal vote and an equal voice. Anyone can work hard and achieve success. Any child can become president. At least that's the theory. The reality can be quite different.

When the country was founded, it was controlled by white, Protestant men who owned property. Later, the right to vote was extended to most white men. Women gained the right to vote in 1920. The Fifteenth Amendment gave African Americans the right to vote in 1870, yet discriminatory policies often prevented them from acting on that right. Congress enacted the Voting Rights Act of 1965 to prevent this discrimination. Still, poor people—often mainly racial minorities and people with disabilities—may face barriers to voting. Their voices may not be heard.

The American Dream promises that anyone who works hard enough can achieve success. In financial terms, success is often defined as the ability to earn good money. Although hard work increases one's chance of financial success, achieving the dream is far easier for some groups than for others.

People who start in the middle or upper classes have the best chance of financial success. Many factors play into this. Children whose parents are financially well-off typically have better health care. They attend good schools with advanced classes. After-school activities provide even more opportunities for learning. When these children graduate from high school, their parents can usually afford to help pay for college. After college, the parents' connections can help these young people find jobs.

On the other hand, poor children may not receive proper health care. They may live in old buildings that make them sick and cause behavior and learning problems. Their schools may be overcrowded and underfunded. Their parents may not have the resources to supplement their learning. They can't afford to help pay for higher education. In fact, they may need their children to start work as soon as possible, to help support the family.

People of any race can live in poverty. People of any race can be found in the middle and upper classes. However, due to centuries of racism, some races suffer more poverty than others. In 2016, 8.8 percent of non-Hispanic white Americans lived in poverty, along with 10.1 percent of Asian Americans. In contrast, 22 percent of African Americans and 19.4 percent of Hispanics lived in poverty. For Native Americans, more than a quarter live below the federal poverty line.

Under the law, everyone should have an equal chance to get a good education, find a good job, and be paid well. However, in reality, educational funding tends to keep richer communities successful. Meanwhile it prevents students in poor communities from getting out of poverty. Because poverty is tied to race, race is still a factor in economic success in America. Race can also affect income, housing, medical care, and even life expectancy.

Other factors contribute to a lack of freedom, opportunity, or even basic safety. Women make less money than men for the same jobs, even when they have equal education and experience. Women are also more often victims of sexual harassment on the job and elsewhere. They are less likely to receive proper health care. In addition, women face higher risks of being victims of domestic and sexual violence. Native and indigenous men and women are more often victims of violence than other races, with over 81 percent suffering violence in their lifetimes. LGBTQ+ people are also disproportionately the victims of violence, including murder.

Conditions such as these have led many marginalized groups to demand more rights. Some groups band together based on a particular identity, such as race, religion, gender identity, or gender expression. They take political action based on this identity. Critics of identity politics often claim it divides people, causing us to focus on our differences rather than our similarities. Some say we should ignore race and gender in politics because the true struggle is between the poor working class against the rich elite. Some critics even blame identity politics for the Democrats' loss of the 2016 election. The Democrats did not appeal enough to the majority white working class, they suggest. Meanwhile, Donald Trump appealed to the identity politics of that particular group.

Advocates of identity politics say that recognizing different identities gives voices to people who have been ignored. It can lead to important political and social changes. For someone who feels left out of society, joining a group whose members share an identity can provide valuable bonding.

A person may be discriminated against due to race, class, gender identity, sexual orientation, physical or mental conditions, religion, and other factors. Some people may identify with a single disadvantaged group. Yet other people may be oppressed in multiple ways. In the 1970s, African American women faced racism in the feminist movement and sexism in the civil rights movement. They began to call for a form of black feminism. This attempted to combat the different forms of oppression faced by women of color.

In 1989, law professor and social theorist Kimberlé Crenshaw gave a new name to this concept. *Intersectionality* refers to the connected, overlapping, or intersecting nature of social categories. Intersectionality acknowledges that people may be affected by several disadvantages or forms of discrimination. People who face two or more forms of oppression have different experiences than people facing only one form.

Can intersectionality help us understand and appreciate each other better? Can it help those facing multiple forms of oppression finally achieve equality? Or do politics based on identity divide people? Will we only achieve true equality when we ignore individual differences? Is that even possible? The current debate is explored in *Introducing Issues with Opposing Viewpoints: Intersectionality and Identity Politics*, shedding light on this ongoing, complex issue.

Chapter 1

What's the Goal of Intersectionality and Identity Politics?

Can we find common ground at the intersection of our identities?

Intersectionality Should Be Integrated into Social Issues

Leigh Chandler

"The theory has proven necessary to understanding a wide range of difference."

In the following viewpoint, Leigh Chandler explains what intersectionality means. Chandler begins by discussing the concept's history and its importance. She then offers suggestions for gaining more understanding and experience with the concept. The author argues that it is not enough that intersectionality exist as a concept; rather, it must be put into practice with the goal of promoting equality. Chandler is the Fund Development and Communications Associate for YW Boston. YW Boston works toward racial, gender, and social equality in Boston, Massachusetts.

AS YOU READ, CONSIDER THE FOLLOWING QUESTIONS:
1. How can someone be disadvantaged by multiple sources of oppression, according to the author?
2. How did the idea of intersectionality arise from the experiences of African American women?
3. What are some ways to learn more about intersectionality, according to the article?

"What is intersectionality, and what does it have to do with me?" by Leigh Chandler, YWCA Boston, March 29, 2017. Reprinted by permission.

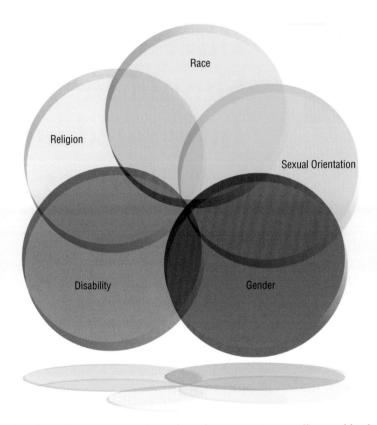

Intersectionality is the interconnectedness of social categorizations, as illustrated by this Venn diagram.

H ere at YW Boston, intersectionality is central to the work we do.

We know that everyone reading this has come to follow YW Boston's work from different entry points. Some of us hold female empowerment close to heart, perhaps seeking a more equitable world for ourselves or our daughters. Some of us have experienced racial discrimination personally, perhaps through generations of our family. Some of us have little experience with social justice, but seek a better understanding of inequity in Greater Boston. All of us seek change in our community, no matter how we became involved.

Despite our shared vision, social equity work can oftentimes feel exclusionary to those who are not familiar with the lingo. Intersectionality, in particular, is a term that many people and organizations assert an importance for, but that others are unclear on.

Understanding the terminology used in equity work is a useful tool for people expanding their knowledge on the issues they care about.

If you've ever scratched your head when a friend, colleague, or writer has spoken of intersectionality (or you'd like to deepen your understanding of the theory), this post is for you.

What Is It and Where Does It Come From?

Intersectionality, *n.* The interconnected nature of social categorizations such as race, class, and gender, regarded as creating overlapping and interdependent systems of discrimination or disadvantage; a theoretical approach based on such a premise. (Oxford Dictionary)

Intersectionality is a framework for conceptualizing a person, group of people, or social problem as affected by a number of discriminations and disadvantages. It takes into account people's overlapping identities and experiences in order to understand the complexity of prejudices they face.

In other words, intersectional theory asserts that people are often disadvantaged by multiple sources of oppression: their race, class, gender identity, sexual orientation, religion, and other identity markers. Intersectionality recognizes that identity markers (e.g. "female" and "black") do not exist independently of each other, and that each informs the others, often creating a complex convergence of oppression. For instance, a black man and a white woman make $0.74 and $0.78 to a white man's dollar, respectively. Black women, faced with multiple forms of oppression, only make $0.64. Understanding intersectionality is essential to combatting the interwoven prejudices people face in their daily lives.

Kimberlé Crenshaw, law professor and social theorist, first coined the term intersectionality in her 1989 paper "Demarginalizing the Intersection of Race and Sex: A Black Feminist Critique of Antidiscrimination Doctrine, Feminist Theory and Antiracist Politics." The theory emerged two decades earlier, however, when black feminists began to speak out about the white, middle-class nature of the mainstream feminist movement. Many black women found it difficult to identify with the issues of the mainstream (white) feminist movement, issues such as the pressure to be a homemaker. Black women, who often had to work in order to keep their family afloat and therefore did not have the luxury of being homemakers, did not feel as though these issues pertained to their experiences. At the same time, many black women experienced sexism while participating in the Civil Rights movement and were often shut out of leadership positions. This intersectional experience of facing racism in the feminist movement and sexism in civil rights encouraged black women to call for a feminist practice that centralized their lived experiences.

The Combahee River Collective, a black feminist lesbian organization, released the Combahee River Collective Statement in 1978 to define and encourage black feminism. In the introduction these women state that "The synthesis of these oppressions creates the conditions of our lives. As Black women we see Black feminism as the logical political movement to combat the manifold and simultaneous oppressions that all women of color face." They fought not only for representation in both the Civil Rights and feminist movements, but also for recognition as black women, rather than just black or just female individuals.

Crenshaw expanded on the Collective's theory, stating that in order to understand the oppression of black women, it is necessary to look at the intersection of blackness and womanhood. While many who championed intersectionality early on were African American women, the theory has proven necessary to understanding a wide range of difference, including individuals' sexual orientation, age, class, disability, and more.

Nowadays, intersectionality is considered crucial to social equity work. Activists and community organizations are calling for and participating in more dynamic conversations about the differences in experience among people with different overlapping identities. Without an intersectional lens, events and movements that aim to address injustice towards one group may end up perpetuating systems of inequities towards other groups. Intersectionality fully informs YW Boston's work, by encouraging nuanced conversations around inequity in Boston. It enlightens us to health disparities among women of color, provides pathways for our youth leaders to understand identity, and is crucial to the advocacy work we support.

What Can I Do?

Intersectionality may seem theoretical, but it is meant to be utilized. No matter how or when you have become involved with equity work, it is always possible to more fully integrate intersectionality into your view of these issues.

Is your work toward social equity intersectional? Check out these tips and reflect:

Recognize difference

Oftentimes, it is easier to believe and to explain to others that "all women feel" a certain way or that "LGBTQ+ people believe" some common understanding, but this does not reflect reality. We must recognize that all unique experiences of identity, and particularly ones that involve multiple overlapping oppressions, are valid.

Do not shy away from recognizing that people experience the world differently based on their overlapping identity markers. Because of the way we have been socialized to continue feeding systems of oppression, we often feel it is rude to formally recognize others' difference. We see this in how people are uncomfortable naming another person's perceived race or asking for someone's preferred pronouns. However, we must recognize these identities as a way to step beyond our assumptions that our experience is common. One way of doing so is when you attend rallies, take a look at the signs that others hold —how do they assert their identity and how does this inform the issues they care most about?

Avoid oversimplified language

Once we recognize this difference, we can move away from language that seeks to define people by a singular identity. You may have heard after the Women's March that many trans folks and allies felt uncomfortable with the vagina-centric themes of the march. Assuming that all women have vaginas or are defined by their bodies is an oversimplification that erases the experiences of those who exist beyond the gender binary. By avoiding language that assumes our own experiences are baseline, we can open ourselves up to listening to others' points of view.

Analyze the space you occupy

Becoming comfortable recognizing difference also involves recognizing when that difference is not represented in the spaces you occupy. Diversity of all kinds matter in your workplace, your activism, your community spaces, and more. If you are meeting with a local LGBTQ+ organization, is there representation of LGBTQ+ people of color? You may feel that your workplace is racially and ethnically diverse, but is it accessible to people with disabilities? Take note of the welcoming or distancing practices of the spaces you frequent.

Seek other points of view

Explore the narratives of those with different interlocking identities than you. This includes surrounding yourself with others with differing interwoven identities, but keep in mind that oftentimes, even when you have a diverse group of people in an activist space, it falls on people to educate others about the oppressions they face. When these people share their experiences, take the opportunity to listen. However, do not expect people with identity markers other than your own to be there or to want to educate others. In your own time, seek out existing intersectional narratives, from your podcasts to your television. If you are unsure about a concept or want to learn more about a specific intersection of identity, Google it! This will help you be better prepared to enter into conversations with others and progress together.

Show up

Do not expect people who face different systems of oppression than you to rally for causes you care about if you do not rally for theirs.

As you hear about issues others face, learn about the work that is currently being done around these topics. Listen and defer to those who live with these intersectional identities each day. As you do, you will likely deepen your understanding of your own identity and the subjects you care about most.

EVALUATING THE AUTHOR'S ARGUMENTS:

In this viewpoint, author Leigh Chandler claims intersectionality is important and beneficial. Does she provide evidence for this? Does her explanation lead you to agree with her? Why or why not?

Focus on Sameness, Not Differences

James Devereaux

"Maybe identifying an injustice to a group helps diagnose, but identifying sameness cures the ill."

In the following viewpoint, James Devereaux argues against politics based on identity. The author suggests that identity politics gathers people based on their outward appearance rather than their inner beliefs. He calls this heuristic. A heuristic technique is an approach that is practical and fulfills immediate goals but may not be perfect or ideal. Devereaux suggests that politicians use identity politics because it is quicker and easier than explaining complex situations. He suggests a better force for good would be to focus on how people are the same, and thus deserve the same freedoms. In his view, identity politics lack the bonding that comes from recognizing a common human identity. Devereaux is an attorney who often writes for The Foundation for Economic Education.

AS YOU READ, CONSIDER THE FOLLOWING QUESTIONS:
1. What is the danger of focusing on people's differences, according to the author?
2. How could identity politics divide people?
3. How can identity politics encourage stereotypes?

In 2016, a group of students on the UC Berkeley campus physically blocked other students from passing through the iconic Sather Gate, barring the path to anyone not considered to be part of a minority class. Some students were told to walk the long way around despite their effort to be otherwise uninvolved.

Unfortunately, this is but one example—on campuses and in the streets—of a rise in identity politics.

Does a sentiment such as "black power" work to bolster a particular group's identity, or does it divide people?

Groupthink

Identity politics is best described as organizing politically based on identity as opposed to ideas. If this sounds tribal that's because it is.

Political organization often relies on information shortcuts, such as heuristics, to signal and gather like-minded people into groups. Unlike a market, a political economy has no price system to provide information to participants. Instead, by and large, we rely on interest-based coalitions to convey information.

At times those coalitions form less around ideas and more around personal identities. The major problem with identity politics is the fact that it treats outward identity as an information surrogate for inner politics.

Think of how freedom advocacy is often mistaken as a "dog-whistle" or code for distasteful brands of identity politics, such as white identity politics. Or similarly, consider the Salon headline, Libertarianism is for White Men: The Ugly Truth about the Right's Favorite Movement (Which is rather inaccurate).

Even the liberty-oriented can be sympathetic to identity politics.

Jacob Levy of the Niskanen Center, articulated his defense, asserting that identity politics are a useful element in liberalization.

I remain skeptical that it is a tool for liberalism. In fact, since it is treated as an information surrogate it is likely to backfire and work against liberty.

True, we find many examples of oppressed groups binding together under a common banner, but these movements have also appealed to a more common sympathy when increasing liberty—that of our inherent sameness. (In fairness Levy did not dispense with an appeal to universal principles.)

Beware of "Sameness"

We can find many examples in history of impassioned liberty and equality-under-law movements advocating the inherent sameness between the oppressed and downtrodden and the more privileged.

Examples abound in history: The phrase inscribed on an abolitionist coin, "Am I Not a Man and a Brother," or the tireless advocacy of Wilbur Wilberforce, who was said to appeal to the "feelings and humanity" of others when imploring that the slave trade be abolished, or Martin Luther King Jr's impassioned speeches for equality——all appealed to the sameness despite the differences.

This is a powerful argument that is lost in much of the heightened identity politics of today, an element that cannot be dispensed in any political movement if it is to successfully move toward liberalization.

One poignant example of finding political sameness was the alliance between the religious of Exeter Hall and the early economists in 19th century England.

The opposing political faction, including notables such as Thomas Carlyle, John Ruskin, and Charles Dickens, derided the former slave population and their progeny. Carlyle went so far as to claim re-enslavement was necessary to protect and care for this newly freed community—racism and oppression in the guise of paternal care.

However, the religious abolitionists of Exeter Hall and the economists, such as John Mills, insisted that the former slave population was essentially the same as the white population. For the religious, we were all born brothers and sisters, descendants from the same first parents.

For the economists, all people act according to underlying incentives and our basic human nature is the same—only the institutions differed. Carlyle and his allies critiqued this approach responding that economics was a "dismal science" as it purported that the best policy was one that "let a man alone."

Much of this debate continued in the US and into the 20th century, where the progressive movement made similar arguments as Carlyle when evaluating the differences between varied groups.

Many policies arose for those deemed "inferior" such as minority communities and the "feeble-minded." One such example was the acceptance of eugenics, which often advocated for the elimination of undesired characteristics, including perceived low intelligence.

This culminated in the forced sterilization of thousands in the United States. This historic shame is tragically represented in the Supreme Court case *Buck v. Bell*, where it was arrogantly declared that "three generations of imbeciles are enough."

As before, forgoing sameness leads to potentially dangerous paths, and fails to communicate the broader principles of freedom. Current identity politics lack the bonding agent of a common human identity.

In political discourse, substituting identity with policy has led to some being unjustly labeled as bigoted, sexist, or racist since a policy or position has unintentionally (or intentionally) become code for a group identity. It has also distracted from real problems with bigots, sexists, and racists.

Further encouraging identity politics will drive the demand up. As a result, we should expect the value of certain identities to increase, the quantity of different identity groups to multiply, and the division along identities to deepen.

To be clear, it is often true that when state power has infringed on freedoms, or when segments of society have borne a disproportionate weight of government intrusion and force, we will hear about it primarily through the complaints of coalesced interest groups.

And when that oppression is designed to target identity groups the political incentive is for these individuals to identify with those in a similar situation, which will be, in those instances, identity-based.

However, identifying sameness matters more than differences. Maybe identifying an injustice to a group helps diagnose, but identifying sameness cures the ill.

In fact, there are current laws that were once implemented based, at least in part, on identity-driven animus—though it is hardly known now. The War on Drugs and the minimum wage are just two such examples.

Thomas Leonard's "Illiberal Reformers" details how many of these laws originated, some of which continue to receive wide support today. Many of these laws are currently supported by those who, as a result, suffer from them most. The reality is most are unaware of the illiberal origins and the current disproportionate impact.

An Enemy of Liberty

Which brings us back to the initial problem of treating identity as an information surrogate. When combined with vast political ignorance, it becomes dangerous.

A few, such as Bryan Caplan, Ilya Somin, and Jason Brennan, have observed the ubiquitousness of political ignorance and the impact on our politics.

This ignorance is understandable, policy is complex, broad, and time-consuming to understand. Because of the inherent complexity of politics, encouraging identity-based advocacy to create and institute change is likely to exacerbate the ignorance and draw stronger lines between identity groups, thereby increasing the tendency to treat identity as a surrogate for political knowledge. This encourages suspicion of those who appear different instead of seeking information and education.

Sadly, relying on identity politics encourages stereotypes, thwarts the work of freedom, and assigns motives to many without direct evidence. As this occurs, many may eventually conclude: why bother with evidence when we have decided that identity politics is an acceptable surrogate for actual information? And when it is clear that the value of an idea is no longer relevant, and evidence and arguments are substituted with identities, expect unseemly movements to form in response.

Those sympathetic to liberty should then veer away from identity politics, it works against freedom and equality.

EVALUATING THE AUTHOR'S ARGUMENTS:

Viewpoint author James Devereaux argues that we should be focusing on our similarities and not our differences. He views equality as coming from the essential sameness of all people. How does his view contrast with the previous author's? Does one seem more valid than the other, or could both somehow be correct?

Struggling Groups Can Be Stronger Together

"Identity politics when practised correctly does not divide, it simply takes a more nuanced view."

Andrew Galvin

In the following viewpoint, Andrew Galvin offers his response to a published opinion piece. To express his view, he quotes from the earlier piece and responds to different points. The author argues that class struggle (conflict between different classes, such as rich and poor) intersects with other struggles. He believes all struggling groups can support each other. He especially mentions the value of women to activism and calls for men to listen more to women in their activist groups. Galvin is an Irish poet, playwright, and performer. He wrote this piece for Medium, a website that allows authors to express their viewpoints.

AS YOU READ, CONSIDER THE FOLLOWING QUESTIONS:

1. Can someone from the working class be considered privileged, according to the author?
2. In the author's view, do identity politics necessarily divide people?
3. What is false authority and why is it a problem when making an argument?

"Men of the Left vs Intersectionality: A Response," by Andrew Galvin, Medium, May 26, 2017. Reprinted by permission.

Some have suggested that the 2017 "Unite the Right" rally was a reaction to the gains made by various identity groups and the resulting perceived loss of power by white males.

A recent opinion piece in *The Irish Times* took it upon itself to call out culture (yes without a hint of irony) and strike a blow against Identity Politics/Intersectional Feminism. This article is an attempt to draw out and analyse some of the irrationalities, logical inconsistencies, and fallacies contained in the piece.

> *Although he might also be straight, white and male, it would be perverse to describe Ballymun native and founder of Home Sweet Home Dean Scurry as "privileged"*

Now, I don't know Dean Scurry in any way shape or form (beyond the great work he has done with Home Sweet Home) so I will be abstracting him from the argument to try and ensure no disrespect. The inference here seems to be that working class straight white males who have overcome great difficulties can never be described as privileged, and that indeed it would be "perverse" to do so.

This is a common issue and it is grounded in a disparity in our definitions of privilege: If you view privilege and oppression purely through the lens of class (binary), then yes, it is impossible for a working class person to be described as privileged.

If however you view privilege and oppression through an intersectional lens (non-binary) then you integrate many lenses of identity and experience (including class!) and assert that each of us lies on a spectrum of privilege/oppression in each of these areas, privileged in some, oppressed in others. Then through this lens it *is* possible to argue that a working class person holds some privilege in some area/s.

> If the CIA or MI5 wanted to encourage a style of "activism" that could consume an infinite amount of energy, yet was utterly ineffective at anything other than dividing people, it would be the prominence of this very type of politics.

Here the author contends that identity politics is, "utterly ineffective at anything other than dividing people" An absolute statement that requires one contrary example to disprove it so I'll just mention the Marriage Equality movement in Ireland where LGBTQ+ activists led and won a long and sustained political campaign to legally legitimise their marital unions and ensure equal rights.

> We need politics that unites us in our shared humanity, for the 99.9 per cent to come together and fight the 0.1 per cent who are stealing the wealth of the Earth, pitting the poor against the poor and entrapping us in ignorance. We do not need politics that explicitly sets out to divide us and perfectly mirrors what it claims to oppose.

Identity politics when practised correctly does not divide, it simply takes a more nuanced view. Are we being divisive when we speak of atomic structure? We are capable of understanding issues from different viewpoints and at different levels of complexity, so let's do that. I highly recommend this lecture by Kimberle Crenshaw which explains it all very succinctly.

> *Proponents of this ideology demand:*
>
> *Intellectual dishonesty*
>
> *Faith over reason*
>
> *Disdain for evidence*
>
> *That challenges be condemned as blasphemy*
>
> *Their own liturgy*
>
> *Strict orthodoxy*
>
> *Public displays of adherence*
>
> *And most shamefully, the regular public flagellation of heretics.*

One of the biggest problems with this piece is its tendency to state views as fact without any supporting evidence. In fact at this point the author dispenses with any attempt in regard to narrative prose and supporting argument and simply lists a series of damning judgements, procured we can only assume from negative social media interactions, because the author understands intersectional feminism/identity politics better than its own proponents.

Look at the language closely here, "Proponents of this ideology demand." The author is not delineating here between some proponents or many proponents of this ideology. The author simply states that proponents of this ideology demand all the elements of the subsequent list of awfulness. A ridiculous assertion, even if it were accompanied by evidence since it requires only one contrary example to dispute it.

> *Unlike those who need an ever-expanding lexicon to express their beliefs, what I believe can be summed up in one word: equality. We should all be subject to the same laws, all have the same opportunities, all have the same rights, all have the same responsibilities and all be able to use the same language. Now that's something worth fighting for.*

This is essentially an argument against nuance and subtlety. As if an "ever-expanding lexicon" is by nature less truthful or necessary. Simplicity as de-facto supreme attribute. There are times where our language must expand to accommodate the issue we are discussing. By the author's assessment surgeons need only treat "sicknesses" of the "body" and any attempt to communicate more deeply by subdividing both further by describing the specific type of malady and its locus in the body is somehow exclusionary.

> *Postscript? My mate Eric happens to be black and wear his hair in dreads. John Connors actually spent time with the Lakota tribe, who love this use of the term "pow wow." Like me, both John and Eric have overcome an awful lot in their lives. And they don't don the mantle of oppression just to belittle or exclude others.*

The author's big reveal! You know back there, when the author said that his friend Eric agreed with him about how silly the idea of cultural appropriation is, well, Eric's black. Checkmate humourless, feminist, buzz killers! And … and remember back when he mentioned that his mate Dean Scurry was getting grief on twitter about using the phrase "Pow Wow" well, guess what. The author's other mate knows some Lakota tribespeople who reckon it's grand. Boom! In your face, identity politics idiots.

This is the logical fallacy called false authority. Just because I can quote black people who say racism doesn't exist, or that it's cool for white people to use the n-word, or a woman who maintains misogyny is a fantasy created by man-hating feminists, doesn't make it so.

A Case for the Author and a Path Forward

Are there people in the world who act as the author describes. Yes, there are. Are there issues to be dealt with in how some feminists act in the world. I think there are. Just as there are shortfalls in all ideologies themselves and in their application in the world. But to tar all with the one brush is seldom truthful or helpful.

I understand the author's views somewhat I think because I once held them. In my early twenties I would have more or less agreed with him on feminism as a repressive force against men and particularly its perceived silence on class issues. It's a seductive viewpoint. It requires no self-analysis. It is easier to fight for the status-quo than change after all. Since then I have received an invaluable education. A gift from many, generous women. I naturally empathised with the plight of men but thanks to the time and efforts of a multitude of great women, both online and in person, and my own willingness to step into the discomfort that comes with the knowledge of the unearned advantages I hold (just like the author, white male was not an identity I chose but it doesn't stop me benefiting from it) I fostered some empathy for women's experience of this world.

I experienced the justice system in Ireland with regard to sexual assault when an intimate partner was raped, and was forever changed by that. That lead me to discuss the issue with other female friends and future partners. What I discovered horrified me. I am not overstating when I say that I have almost no female friends who have not been sexually assaulted. This lead to similar discussions around intimate partner abuse. I am not overstating when I say that I have almost no female friends who have not been in abusive relationships (abuse is more than just physical violence, it includes emotional, psychological, economic, financial, sexual abuse etc.)

And this lead to similar discussions around structural inequalities, and on, and on, and on … To be clear I would never suggest that the author does not share these understandings or experiences. I acknowledge for example that the author is a vocal and hardworking activist on a broad range of issues, and I respect that. But I would say that this article in particular does not demonstrate the understanding I speak of.

To Men Who Struggle with the #coponcomrades Message
Focus does not equal exclusion. Black lives matter does not presume that all lives do not. A focus on women's issues does not deny that Men suffer also. Intersectional feminism is not the enemy. It is simply a newer, more nuanced map of how oppressions interact in the world, as opposed the reductive identity politics of the class struggle which admits only a singular identity.

A woman's revolution does not undermine the broader revolution. Quite the opposite. It strengthens it. It empowers it. It fuels it. And frankly it is impossible to proceed without it in my view. It is uncomfortable to you. I entirely understand that. Facing your failings. Your faulty narratives. Your part in structures of oppression. The binary simplicity of class struggle can be comforting to those on the right side of the divide while the complexities of intersectionality asks us to acknowledge that as the #coponcomrades message puts it, "We all have to examine ourselves as oppressor as well as oppressed—because we are all both."

At this point hundreds of women across all class divides, races, nationalities, sexual orientations etc. have signed a clear declaration that there is a problem within activist circles. And overwhelmingly the response from men has been dismissive and defensive. It doesn't have to be this way. It is entirely unhelpful to respond this way. Their message is in my view rational, balanced, and delivered with an honour and dignity that stands in stark contrast to the treatment they have received.

Your sisters have a very important message for you and I implore you to listen. Drop the bravado. Drop the ego. Drop the desire to defend your viewpoint. Drop the need to be right. Drop the misrepresentation of the arguments. Be the bigger person if that's how you need to see it. But please don't dig your heels. Imagine for a moment that they have something to say that will benefit us all.

EVALUATING THE AUTHOR'S ARGUMENTS:

In this viewpoint, Andrew Galvin challenges another's opinion piece. Which of the authors provides the most logical, compelling argument? How might your experience and opinions be different if you had only read the original piece?

Viewpoint
4

Identity Politics Will Destroy Democracy

Daniel Wild and Andrew Bushnell

"The final danger of identity politics, then, is that it provides another rationalisation for a state that will not leave us alone."

In the following viewpoint, Daniel Wild and Andrew Bushnell argue that identity politics are divisive. They claim that identity politics condemns ideas such as freedom of speech and the rule of law, because these things are seen as reflecting the interests of the wealthy. They hint that oppressed groups compete for which of them is most oppressed. The authors suggest that supporting and promoting diversity requires ending democracy; identity politics lead to a government that will control every aspect of people's lives. They call for the rejection of identity politics. Wild and Bushnell are Research Fellows at The Institute of Public Affairs, a conservative public policy think tank in Australia.

AS YOU READ, CONSIDER THE FOLLOWING QUESTIONS:
1. Identity politics is an expansion of what socioeconomic analysis, according to the viewpoint?
2. Which specific structures of oppression are mentioned by the authors?
3. From which national perspective do the authors write?

"How Identity Politics Divides Us," by Daniel Wild and Andrew Bushnell, The Institute of Public Affairs, October 10, 2017. Reprinted by permission.

Drawing in people from diverse backgrounds and identity groups acts to minimize a hierarchical structure of privilege and oppression.

The idea that Indigenous Australians should have a separate voice in our Parliament, the push to make Australia Day a representation of our divisions rather than our unity, and the calls for formalised diversity quotas are all manifestations of identity politics, where our legal rights are allocated according to our race, gender and sexuality. This identity politics movement seeks to divide us, and poses a threat to the functioning of our liberal democracy.

Identity politics alleges that our institutions do not treat people equally and perpetuate privilege and oppression. Privilege is defined as unearned advantage gained by membership of a historically powerful group, while oppression is being subject to constraints on one's liberty because of membership of a historically disadvantaged group. Oppression and privilege are created not just by political institutions, but cultural phenomena like the use of language and the "construction" of identity.

Identity politics is an expansion of the Marxist analysis of class, where society is seen as a zero-sum contest for power between the privileged and the oppressed. The Italian theorist Antonio Gramsci, an early proponent of this kind of analysis, argued that, "The marginalised groups of history include not only the economically oppressed, but also women, racial minorities and many 'criminals.'" Just as the proletariat is at the mercy of the predatory capitalist class, other groups in society are unable to live freely while their social context is constrained by the preferences and institutional power of other groups.

This analysis takes as given that evidence of the differential impact of state action on various groups is itself evidence of the hegemony of a privileged elite. For example, the racial bias of Australia's criminal justice system is revealed in the disproportionately-high rate of incarceration of Indigenous Australians.

Identity politics argues that our established values, customs and history do not represent the diverse racial, cultural, and gender identities of Australians. Oppression is seen as an innate feature of the very concepts and language used in the dominant culture. Everything from the fundamentals of liberal democracy such as freedom of speech and the rule of law, the iconography of the nation, and even the everyday language of the people, is condemned for reflecting only the interests of the wealthy and powerful, and oppressing women, members of minority races and cultures, and the economically disadvantaged.

The structures of oppression—racism, sexism, classism and so on—created by our biased institutions interact with one another, creating a hierarchy of privilege and oppression, in a dynamic sometimes referred to as "intersectionality." In response to aggregate group differences, members of oppressed groups are motivated to see their political interests as tied to their identities, and to vote as blocs.

Identity groups are encouraged to cooperate with one another for tactical advantage, although this cooperation is not always smooth as there are internal conflicts as to which group is the more oppressed. In theory, though, they are united in a vision of a world of radical liberation, in which their identities, and the oppression on which they are founded, melt into air.

Proponents argue that our institutions oppress the people who share these identities, who are all morally required to fight back against them. Consider a recent exchange between *The Guardian* journalist Katharine Murphy and a counterpart from *The West Australian*, Sarah Martin at the National Press Club. As part of a panel discussion, Martin said that she "considered [herself] a journalist, not a female journalist." Murphy replied, "There is a special place in hell for women who don't help other women." That this is a line first used by former United States Secretary of State Madeleine Albright at a Hillary Clinton rally should surprise no-one.

This demand for group loyalty in the struggle against our political and cultural traditions is incompatible with liberal democracy. Such is the threat it poses to sensible politics, in America there is already a growing realisation among some on the left that identity politics is a dead-end. Left-wing academic Mark Lilla argues in a new book that politics should be about "emphasizing what we all share and owe one another as citizens, not what differentiates us." Socialist senator Bernie Sanders has also made the case that identity politics is an abandonment of the working class. While this is a welcome development, it will prove futile unless it is more widely understood why identity politics is not just politics as usual.

In America, Hillary Clinton's 2016 Presidential campaign provides a vivid example of identity politics in action. Clinton attempted to recreate the coalition that carried Barack Obama to consecutive victories, made up of minority groups, women, young people, and those with university degrees. Clinton rallies were littered with signs displaying "[identity group] for Clinton." "Immigration reform" was designed to win Latino voters, with the assumption that Trump's tougher posture could not appeal to American Latinos. Clinton herself first entered the Democratic Party Convention by breaking a "glass ceiling" and becoming the first female nominee of a major party for president.

In Australia, identity politics can be seen in the bipartisan talking point that Australia's greatness resides in its multiculturalism, by which it is meant that the diversity of identifiers claimed by Australians is somehow more important than the identity that they all share. It can also be seen in the "social justice" campaigning of the country's crony capitalists and sporting organisations. All of these cases are about disestablishing traditional norms, which are held to be in some sense discriminatory.

Political correctness is also a manifestation of identity politics. While there is nothing new about social pressure enforcing social norms, political correctness is a systematic attempt to deconstruct the complex web of meanings connoted with words and symbols to expose hidden prejudices. New taboos are asserted and new usages favoured, with the goal of eliminating connotations that perpetuate disadvantage.

All Australians must reject identity politics, which threatens the breakdown of liberal democracy and an even more powerful and arbitrary state. Instead, we must advocate for our universal institutions and formal equality. Only from there can we cultivate the empathy and mutual trust on which our civilisation depends.

Problems with Identity Politics

Identity politics is revolutionary in its aims. It aspires not to government but to perpetual reign, seeking to replace the established institutions and customs of our country with notions supposedly more democratic and reflective of society's diversity. Identity politics, then, is a far-reaching critique of our entire social order.

There are three main problems with identity politics: it is incompatible with being an individual, it renders impossible the spirit of compromise on which liberal democracy depends, and it demands an expansive, arbitrary state that will manage every aspect of our lives.

First, identity politics takes literally the activist maxim that "the personal is political," and asserts that converse is also true. Every action by an individual either perpetuates oppression or fights it. Every individual who is a member of an oppressed group is himself oppressed, and every individual who is part of the dominant group is himself privileged, no matter the actual experiences he may have had.

In this way identity politics denies the diversity of experiences of individuals within groups, reducing each person to the group identity and ascribing to him the group experience. You can never be more than a member of your identity group.

This perspective also denies us the ability to change our own circumstances. Anyone who thinks that the identity politics-defined context does not apply to him is guilty of false consciousness, apparently unable to know his own mind.

Second, by locating politics at the level of between-group conflict, rather than as an activity engaged in by individuals for their own purposes, identity politics weakens the possibility of political compromise.

Public policy becomes a matter of life and death for each individual self—this leads to the left's routine conflation of their supposed political oppression and violence. This is used to excuse its own violence, as seen in the attack on Andrew Bolt earlier this year and in the riots on American university campuses.

Because the self is constructed by the realities of structural oppression, it can only be understood by those who have experienced the same forces. Only in-group members can properly understand the interests of the group. The experience of oppression cannot be understood by those who are privileged, and because of this the privileged cannot justly make suggestions to, let alone rules for, the oppressed.

Recent discontent about "cultural appropriation" and the offensiveness of artists assuming trans-cultural points of view is illustrative. The author Lionel Shriver spoke at the Brisbane Writers Festival in 2016 in defence of authors' right, indeed duty, to draw on the experiences of others, and she noted that without this kind of engagement, there could be no fiction. For this she was subject to the predictable social media storm.

Third, identity politics calls into question liberal democracy itself, and ultimately expands the power of the state.

If empathy is not possible, if it is not possible to creatively engage with and assume the point of view of another, then liberal democracy fails. Indeed, the entire civilising process of abstracting from our own experiences to general social rules fails.

All institutions, including rules, are seen to reflect only the prejudices of those who created them, and those people's interest in retaining and strengthening their own power. Everything is political. This in turn justifies the seizure of power and the elimination of institutions built to disperse or limit it.

In political correctness we can see the corrosive effect of identity politics on community. Our language and our culture bind us together and allow the emergence of the trust upon which liberal democracy depends. Without a shared network of symbols we must always talk past each other. In his invention of Newspeak, George Orwell saw clearly that those who claim authority over the dictionary mean to take possession of the mind itself. The goal of political correctness is ultimately to render the new taboos unthinkable.

Identity politics extends politics to every part of society, eliminating the distinction between public and private. For this reason, identity politics is very different from politics as usual.

Democratic politics has always been based on politicians putting together coalitions of interest groups through the promise of preferential public policy. But it is a false equivalence to see the coalition of identity blocs, defined top-down by Marxian analysis, as the same as, say, the coalition of small business owners, professionals, and farmers coming together to campaign for reduced regulation and taxation. This policy goal can be delivered from within the institutional structure of the country. By contrast, identity politics sees no possibility of compromise.

In this inconsistency, we can see the future of identity politics: an expansive bureaucracy inserting itself into every exchange between individuals and groups, a state based not on rules but on trade-offs, and the constant monitoring of all relations to ensure that they are not "oppressive." It brings to mind the notorious reflection by former head of the Australian Human Rights Commission, Gillian Triggs, that despite extensive restrictions on free speech "sadly you can say what you like around the kitchen table at home." It should be obvious that such ideas cannot coexist with our traditional liberties. The final danger of identity politics, then, is that it provides another rationalisation for a state that will not leave us alone.

Towards a Solution

Taken to its logical conclusion, identity politics poses a threat to the continuation of the liberal democratic order, by indicting not only our existing institutions but the possibility of institutions founded on formal equality—that is, the idea that a rule can and should be applied to all individuals regardless of their socioeconomic circumstances.

The rejection of a rules-based order is mistaken. Identity politics misunderstands individual dignity and democracy. Universal rules secure dignity, and institutions embedded in a complex system of law and custom express collective solidarity rather than suppress it.

Being bound by the same institutions in the same way is an expression of, and reinforces, empathy. The principle of equal justice before the law, for example, assures that each of us, should we be accused of a crime, will be treated as everyone else is treated. And because we each know that everyone is subject to the law in this way, we can rely on one another to behave in certain ways. Institutions such as this one enable us to imagine ourselves in the place of others, and this builds mutual trust.

Similarly, sharing a language and customs strengthens our ties to one another. The norms and expectations embedded in this culture work like the principles of justice to create shared understandings and references, upon which relationships can be built.

Identity politics, by contrast, divides people (who otherwise share an institutional identity) on the basis of aggregate results that mean nothing to specific individuals. This is not a useful exercise. And in any event, it is self-defeating: the remedies for the constructed grievances assume the individual agency and democratic solidarity that identity politics undermines.

The relevant question is not whether our institutions favour particular norms—of course they do—but whether they represent a good faith attempt to secure the rights of everyone subject to them. The freedom and prosperity of our liberal democracy strongly suggests that they do.

However, it will not be enough to defeat identity politics at the ballot box. In defending our existing institutions, we cannot retreat from the defence of our values. Identity politics extends its critique to all aspects of our society, and we must extend our defence to meet its challenge.

At the institutional level, some of the tension created by identity politics can be eased by limiting the influence that national politics has over our lives.

Situating political power in local institutions, closer in geography and custom to the people they represent, would provide more opportunity for people to see their own identities reflected in their political representation, as would increasing the use of direct democratic engagement, like plebiscites.

Over the longer-term, the case for our history and institutions needs to be made in the academy and the popular culture.

The challenge identity politics represents to liberal democracy is genuine, and not easily dismissed. Our nation-state's political and social institutions have emerged from our history and tradition, and establish certain norms that do not exist everywhere in the world.

Liberalism's ambition, as it has been understood for more than two centuries now, has been to bring more and ultimately all of the members of society into the community of meaning that our institutions represent. That ambition is as important now as it has ever been. We need to make the case that liberal democracy remains the best way to protect the rights of all Australians and to secure a stable social order within which individuals can live their own lives.

EVALUATING THE AUTHORS' ARGUMENTS:

In this viewpoint, Daniel Wild and Andrew Bushnell are opposed to identity politics. Compare their views to the second viewpoint in this chapter, which also criticized identity politics. Do they use the same or different reasons? How does each argument use language to sway the reader?

My Feminism Is Stronger When I Listen to the Experiences of Others

"Despite how daunting and intimidating the term intersectionality may seem, it's just about us standing up and looking out for each other."

Taylor Hawk

In the following viewpoint, Taylor Hawk describes how intersectionality affects feminism. She notes that she is a white, straight, able-bodied, middle-class woman. As such, she has fewer challenges than some other women do. By listening to others and trying to understand their experiences, she can get a broader view of the challenges women face. Then she can work toward a feminism that supports all women. Hawk wrote this viewpoint for The Odessey, a crowdsourced media platform.

AS YOU READ, CONSIDER THE FOLLOWING QUESTIONS:

1. Whose issues have been the focus of feminism so far, according to the author?
2. What is "white feminism"?
3. How can people achieve intersectional feminism, according to the sources included here?

"What Is 'Intersectional Feminism'?" by Taylor Hawk, Denison, July 26, 2016. Reprinted by permission.

Women with disabilities are often overlooked in both the feminist and disabled movements. How can individuals who intersect with multiple marginalized groups be heard?

Most know that feminism is the movement set on achieving gender equality. But not as many know what intersectional feminism is. So what is it, exactly? The term intersectionality was coined by civil rights activist and professor Kimberlé Crenshaw and can be defined as "the interconnected nature of social categorizations such as race, class, and gender as they apply to a given individual or group, regarded as creating overlapping and interdependent systems of discrimination or disadvantage." By adding the idea of intersectionality to feminism, the movement becomes truly inclusive, and allows women of all races, economic standings, religions, identities and orientations for their voices to be heard.

Over the course of its existence, feminism has mainly focused on the issues experienced by white, middle-class women. For example, it is largely shared and advertised that a woman makes 78 cents to a man's dollar. But this is only the statistic for white women. As upsetting as it is, women of minority groups make even less. Black women earn 64 cents to white men's dollar and Hispanic women only earn 56 cents. Intersectional feminism takes into account the many different ways each woman experiences discrimination. "White feminism" is a term that is used to describe a type of feminism that overshadows the struggles women of color, LGBTQ women and women of other minority groups face. So, essentially, it's not true feminism at all.

As explained in this video (https://www.huffingtonpost.com/entry/why-we-need-to-talk-about-white-feminism_us_55c8ca-5ce4b0f73b20ba020a), "white feminism" ignores intersectionality and neglects to recognize the discriminations experienced by women who are not white. It's important to note that not all feminists who are white practice "white feminism." "White feminism" depicts the way white women face gender inequality as the way all women experience gender inequality, which just isn't correct.

Unfortunately, celebrities and the media are often guilty of doing this as well. An example of this is the great Nicki Minaj and Taylor Swift debacle of 2015. As Nicki tweeted her disappointment of not being nominated for Video of The Year, she brought to light a very important issue. She pointed out that most music videos nominated only showed white, slender-bodied women. Taylor took this as a personal dig and sent out the now infamous tweet in response. Instead of using her voice to recognize the prevalent problem Nicki was discussing, Taylor became defensive and claimed Nicki was pitting women against women. Eventually, the "feud" came to an end when Nicki had Taylor join her onstage for her performance. But, this exchange can still serve as a reminder of how important intersectionality really is.

The key to combating "white feminism" is education about intersectionality. In an interview, Crenshaw defines intersectionality as, "The idea that we experience life, sometimes discrimination, sometimes benefits, based on a number of identities." She first started to develop her theory on intersectionality when she studied the ways black women are discriminated against for both their gender and race. She comments, "The basic term came out of a case where I was looking at black women who were being discriminated against, not just as black people and not just as women, but as black women. So, intersectionality was basically just a metaphor to say they are facing race discrimination from one direction. They have gender discrimination from another direction, and they're colliding in their lives in ways we really don't anticipate and understand."

So, now that we understand what intersectionality is, how can we incorporate it into our feminism? As explained by Laci Green and Franchesca Ramsey, two awesome Internet ladies, in this video, there can be three easy steps in achieving intersectional feminism. They explain the steps as, "1. Examine our own privilege. 2. Listen to each other. 3. Practice feminism through a broader, more inclusive lens."

It's crucial to check your own privilege in society in order to be a better feminist. I, for example, am a white, straight, able-bodied, middle-class woman. This means that I personally don't have to face challenges that other women do. So, it's important that I recognize my privilege and listen to women who experience the world differently than I do. As Laci says in the video, "On the feminist issues where we hold privilege, it's crucial to listen to women who don't. To listen to their experiences, to see the world through a more complex lens and to raise the voices of those who have less power." Franchesca adds, "You can't exactly walk the walk if you have no idea where the walk even goes." Despite how daunting and intimidating the term intersectionality may seem, it's just about us standing up and looking out for each other.

Intersectionality is a term used to describe how different factors of discrimination can meet at an intersection and can affect someone's life. Adding intersectionality to feminism is important to the movement because it allows the fight for gender equality to become inclusive. Using intersectionality allows us all to understand each other a little bit better.

At the end of the day, we might all experience discrimination and gender inequality differently and uniquely, but we are all united in our hope for equality.

EVALUATING THE AUTHOR'S ARGUMENTS:

Viewpoint author Taylor Hawk quotes several sources in her piece. Review the article to note where she expresses her own opinion and where she quotes others. What effect does this balance have on the overall strength of the viewpoint? Do you think it would be weaker or stronger if she only shared her own opinions?

Chapter 2

Will Intersectionality Unite or Divide People?

Can people with different struggles work toward the same goals?

Work Against Oppression, not for Your Group

> "We have
> the ability,
> if we choose
> to use this,
> to truly
> challenge the
> culture to
> move forever
> forward
> and to grow
> by looking
> beyond just
> ourselves."

Dr. Warren J. Blumenfeld

In the following viewpoint, Dr. Warren J. Blumenfeld argues that people vary greatly, even within a single identity community. Still, people joining movements based on identity have successfully worked toward political and social change for that group. He uses the LGBTQ movement as an example. While working together on some issues, splinter groups and individuals may have wildly different outlooks. Therefore, in the author's view, identity politics is limited in what it can do. Blumenfeld sees more value in politics based on ideas or philosophies rather than on identity. This allows individual differences for people with similar goals. His ultimate goal is to dismantle oppression, which is a goal that can unite people with many different identities. Blumenfeld is an author and editor with an interest in social justice and LGBTQ issues.

  1. How does the author use the metaphor of people being like snowflakes?
  2. How can people from the same identity group still have very different viewpoints?
  3. What are some examples of oppressed groups that may have similar goals?

I often hear a saying in my Jewish community that "Whenever there are two Jews in a room, there will be a least three different opinions."

People tell me a similar saying circulates in their various communities, and it underscores a crucial point in that every overall demographic group stands not as a unified, like-minded, like-opinionated, and monolithic block in terms of political, social, spiritual, and economic strategic agendas, but rather, as enormously diverse with internally contradictory and vastly opposing positions on the full array of topics.

If this is true, then how have people in a United States context who share a similar social identity come together in alliance and work for their liberation? In other words, how has the concept of "identity politics" been possible?

The Complexity of Humanity

First, this very question fails to address the fact that each person is composed of multiple identity positions that interconnect with each other. Depending on time and location, some of these identities may appear more or less salient, important, or central to the individual. Our society accords some identities more unearned privileges while simultaneously according less to other identities.

Secondly, as no two falling snowflakes appear identical in structure or shape, no two people are born with duplicate internal temperaments or personalities, nor are they exposed to the same exact forms of socialization during their formative and extended years.

The author of this viewpoint believes that identity politics have limited the LGBTQ community from fighting the larger war of oppression.

Each person is, therefore, as unique as a snowflake, regardless of their socially constructed identities.

That said, people have joined in movements around one or a couple of identities, and they have successfully pushed for social, legislative, and political change. For example, lesbians, gay men, bisexuals, and trans* people have come together to increase our visibility in the media and within the larger society.

We have joined in alliance to fight for marriage equality, entrance into military service, equality of treatment in housing, employment, insurance coverage, public accommodations, partnership benefits, adoption, and many others concerns.

We have and continue to work to dismantle the social, medical, and religious stigma that have long plagued our lives and our very existence; we have challenged conditions that place our bodies at risk for random acts of violence; we have worked to end the bullying of our youth in the schools and our workers in the workplace; and we have joined to empower each and every one of us to live with pride, dignity, integrity, and authenticity.

Though the political and theocratic right accuses us of pushing some sort of conspiratorial "gay agenda" on the people of our country, to paraphrase my opening saying: "Whenever there are two queer people in a room, there will be at least three different opinions."

Even the use of the term "queer" has been highly contested within LGBT communities. Some lesbian and gay people don't consider bisexual and pansexual people as part of their communities, while some LGB people would rather trans* people go away and form fully separate communities. Oy vey!

Just look at a few of the enormous array of groups and their "agendas": there are gays for Trump, LGBTQ Marxists, "Log Cabin Republicans," LGBTQ people for Hillary, "Gays Against Guns (GAG)," LGBTQ members of the National Rifle Association, LGBTQ anarchists, LGBTQ Catholics, "Sisters of Perpetual Indulgence," "Ladies Against Women," "Dykes on Bikes," LGBTQ atheists, LGBTQ Muslims, lesbian daughters of Holocaust survivors, LGBTQ Bridge clubs, LGBTQ athletic clubs, Puerto Rican gay men's organizations, black lesbians groups, groups for LGBTQ deaf people and for LGBTQ elders, and yes, even LGBTQ members of racist white nationalist gangs.

Inherent Restrictions

So even though identity politics has served certain of our purposes and has gained us selected victories, with the incredible diversity within LGBTQ communities in terms of social identities and political philosophies and outlooks, identity politics has shown its inherent restrictions. Therefore, its use can only take us to a limited point along our multiple paths.

Though I continue to engage in identity politics occasionally on particular issues, I have come to understand that sexual identities and gender identities and expressions with the social oppressions that come with these are simply not sufficient to connect a community, and by extension, to fuel a movement for progressive social change.

Therefore, my major focus and energy has been to join and connect with people of similar political ideas and ideologies that cut across individuals from disparate social identities in what some call "idea politics."

My motto is: "I don't care who's in your bed. I care instead what's in your head!"

In this conception, people come together with others of like minds, political philosophies, and strategies for achieving their objectives. Though many differences inevitably remain, overall, we read from a similar, if not from the same, page.

Oppression operates like a wheel with many spokes in which each spoke represents one of the virtually endless systems of oppression. In a United States context, for example, individual spokes may represent oppression toward African Americans, recent African immigrants to this country, Mexican immigrants, US-born citizens whose parents immigrated from Cuba, white women, trans* women, gay men, Muslims, atheists, people along the autism spectrum, elders, youth, Spanish as first-language speakers, people outside the current socially-determined parameters of body size, and I could continue endlessly.

I have been joining with people who understand that if we work to dismantle only one or a few specific spokes, the wheel will continue spinning and trampling over people. We are working together toward dismantling all its many hideous spokes in our hopes of one day dismantling oppression in its totality.

So, if indeed it is true, as the old saying goes, that "the fish is the last to see or even feel the water because it is so pervasive," then from our vantage points at the margins or even outside the aquarium, queer people have a special opportunity—indeed, a responsibility—to serve as social commentators, as critics.

Our experiences as outsiders give us the tools to expose and highlight the rigidity, the binary frames, of most social identity categories that flood and saturate our environment. We have the ability, if we choose to use this, to truly challenge the culture to move forever forward and to grow by looking beyond just ourselves.

EVALUATING THE AUTHOR'S ARGUMENTS:

In this viewpoint, the author promotes working across identities to end oppression. This is in contrast to working only for those within one's own identity. Does he make a good case for his viewpoint? What are some benefits and challenges to this philosophy?

Our Identities Are Worth Fighting For

"It's never been more important to continue talking— and arguing, and complaining, and venting— about identity in America."

Tasneem Raja

In the following viewpoint, Tasneem Raja responds to accusations made by analysts and pundits that Democrats paid too much attention to identity politics during the 2016 election, and that is why their candidates lost. As noted in Chapter 1, viewpoint 2, some people believe results such as these indicate that identity politics divide rather than unite. However, Raja feels that ignoring identity politics will allow the majority now in power—straight, white males—to remain the dominant voice in society. Raja is a journalist and editor. She wrote this viewpoint for National Public Radio, a nonprofit media organization.

AS YOU READ, CONSIDER THE FOLLOWING QUESTIONS:
1. What is the danger in silencing identity politics, according to this author?
2. What examples of identity politics influencing American popular culture are cited?
3. How can complaining and arguing be beneficial, according to the author?

"Commentator: Don't Stop Arguing, Complaining and Fighting For 'Identity Politics,'" by Tasneem Raja, npr, December 8, 2016. Reprinted by permission.

Are identity politics effective, even if they don't translate to election victories? The 2016 US presidential election had people questioning whether they did more harm than good.

In a recent essay in the *New York Times*, Columbia professor and historian Mark Lilla issued a warning to liberals left stunned by President-elect Donald Trump's victory: Knock it off with the "identity politics" or be doomed to repeat this failure.

"American liberalism," he wrote, "has slipped into a kind of moral panic about racial, gender, and sexual identity that has distorted liberalism's message and prevented it from becoming a unifying force capable of governing."

This admonition has been welcomed, and echoed, by pundits and public figures left and right.

"Make identity politics the main operational model in a country that is two-thirds white and 50 percent or so male, and what do you expect?" asked the National Review. Sen. Bernie Sanders warned that the Democratic Party's future rests on whether it can "go beyond identity politics" and says he is "deeply humiliated" by the party's failure to attract more people with his white, working-class background.

No one seems to have a satisfying definition of what "identity politics" means, exactly, but the message is clear: Liberals have been paying too much attention to race and gender and sexual orientation—or not enough attention to the right variants of those—and sensible Americans are rightly saying "no thanks."

The critique is aimed at the astonishingly broad, often fractious, ever-shifting coalition of voices that has been pushing Americans to rethink essentially everything about the way we treat each other. That coalition has been at it in full force for the past few years, on every available platform, from street protests and campus walkouts to tweetstorms and first-person essays; from investigative reports to Hollywood boycotts to a new crop of identity-focused podcasts helmed by prominent writers and thinkers of color.

Make America Great Again?

What Lilla and others keen on pulling the plug on conversations about multiculturalism and diversity don't realize is that by doing so, they play right into the hands of the newly emboldened neo-Nazis who helped put Trump in office and are now delighting over several of his post-election staff and Cabinet picks. Shutting down these conversations—or redirecting them to the concerns of white, straight, mostly male Americans—is precisely what those groups want badly to see happen.

Richard Spencer, the head of the white supremacist National Policy Institute, made it clear in a recent speech at the Ronald Reagan building in Washington, D.C., that the so-called alt-right won't be satisfied by a ban on Muslims or the deportation of millions of immigrants in the US illegally. They want to go back to a time when no one questioned why all the Academy Award winners were white or wondered whether the black man shot by the police officer deserved it; back to a time when even if someone questioned those things, who would listen?

Listen to Spencer boasting to a crowd of about 200 people, most of them white men, some of whom responded with Nazi salutes:

> *Within the very blood in our veins as children of the sun lies the potential for greatness. That is the great struggle we are called to. We are not meant to live in shame and weakness and disgrace. We were not meant to beg for moral validation from some of the most despicable creatures to ever populate the planet. We were meant to overcome. Overcome all of it.*

Neo-Nazis and white supremacists like the ones brazenly applauding that night ("Hail Trump! Hail our people!") long to once again feel safe parading their supposed superiority around without anyone talking back loudly enough to matter. Others worry about being bumped from the head of the line, where, to their ears, terms like "inclusion" and "anti-racism" are code for "white genocide." They all see the emerging Trump administration as a potential partner in creating the country they want to live in, one that preserves their version of white culture.

"I think we can be the ones out in front, thinking about those things [Trump] hasn't quite grasped yet" and pushing for new policies "that have a realistic chance of being implemented," NPI's Spencer told the *New York Times*.

Others point out that with the right guy in charge, you don't need to change the laws to change society.

"A change in tone would be as dramatic as a change in policy because a president and his cabinet have tremendous influence that goes well beyond policy," Jared Taylor, an editor of the self-described "race realism" website American Renaissance, wrote last year. For instance, when it comes to immigration, "white, high-IQ, English-speaking people obviously assimilate best, and someone in a Trump administration might actually say so," Taylor wrote. "A Trump presidency could completely change ... what it means to be an American."

Imperfect Progress

Indeed, rewriting our ideas of what it means to be an American has been the point of all this "identity" politicking all along, and there are signs it's working, albeit slowly, unevenly and imperfectly. For one thing, white supremacists are clearly paying attention. I also take heart in the way words like "institutional racism" and "implicit bias" have become commonplace everywhere from the campaign trail to the *Wall Street Journal.*

Comedians like Hari Kondabalu and Baratunde Thurston and writers like Lindy West and Roxane Gay have made their names by talking about race, gender and identity. Major media outlets like NPR, the Associated Press and the *New York Times* have created newsroom verticals dedicated to the identity beat. The heads of major companies from Marriott to MasterCard have committed to making their staffs and products look more like America. *Vanity Fair* called 2016 "the year Disney started to take diversity seriously," and several of the most anticipated sci-fi and superhero films—typically blindingly white genres—feature people of color in the lead roles.

This progress—this painfully imperfect and unfinished collection of scraps we shine up and call progress—is what a portion of Trump's base wants to undo. Whether or not Lilla and company realize it, they're helping that cause by telling the rest of us to knock off our "fixation" with "identity politics," as though our laser focus has been a fad, not a survival tactic.

That's why it's never been more important to continue talking—and arguing, and complaining, and venting—about identity in America. To continue interrogating whiteness as a construct, even as we discuss the economic woes of many white Americans. To continue asking why so many of our superheroes are white and male, even as we push to better understand the defeat and humiliation felt by many flesh-and-blood white men in our country. To continue surfacing the science that proves this stuff matters: that the faces we see (or don't see) on TV can change our brains; that housing segregation makes some of us scared of each other; that being seen as "other" can hurt your grades, your income, your friendships, even the way you feel about yourself.

We must continue insisting that "identity politics" are simply politics; that a truly civil society requires empathy from all, not self-abnegation of the few; that while it's easy to write off as frivolous and indulgent that which doesn't affect you, doing so doesn't make you a good citizen. Because a logical next step in that direction is writing off entire groups of people whose concerns seem silly to you, or don't make sense to you, or offend you. The neo-Nazis and white supremacists among us are already hard at work trying to make that happen.

Let's not make their jobs any easier.

EVALUATING THE AUTHOR'S ARGUMENTS:

Viewpoint author Tasneem Raja counters claims that identity politics are bad because they divide people. Compare her thoughts to those in Chapter 1, viewpoint 2. Does one of the authors make a stronger case? How so? If both have valid points, how can these concerns be reconciled?

Viewpoint
3

Unite Society Through Diversity

Jason Blakely

"Indeed, the drive for identity recognition is perhaps the most distinctly modern political movement."

In the following viewpoint, Jason Blakely argues that identity politics were used in force by politicians on both sides during the 2016 US presidential election. Identity politics are normally associated with "the left," but they were also used by "right-wing" groups that supported conservative values. These groups included the white working class and even white power groups. This has led some liberals on the left to call for an end to identity politics. The author suggests that a greater awareness of the world's diversity may lead people to feel insecure and call for the elimination of diversity. However, this author believes that diversity must be embraced by everyone. Blakely is an assistant professor of political science at Pepperdine University.

AS YOU READ, CONSIDER THE FOLLOWING QUESTIONS:

1. What is the feature of a modern secular (nonreligious) age, according to the article?
2. How does greater awareness of diversity lead to some people feeling fragile or attacked, according to the author?
3. How long have white men had identity politics, according to this author?

The establishment of identity groups for marginalized individuals, such as Black Lives Matter, may breed a dangerous insecurity in the white working class.

Chris Arnade, a tireless chronicler of white working-class woes, recently wrote: "Most of all, Trump voters want respect ... [but] when they turn on the TV, they see their way of life being mocked and made fun of as nothing but uneducated white trash."

One of the most jarring revelations of the 2016 presidential election was that identity politics—normally associated with the American left—had jumped boundaries and been claimed by the white working and middle class as an ethno-nationalist movement. "Make America Great Again," meant many things to many people, but it undoubtedly included the reassertion of a particular racial and cultural identity within politics.

This surprising turn of events has led some critics to turn on identity politics itself. One is Mark Lilla, a professor of intellectual history at Columbia University, who recently claimed in *The New York Times* that "the age of identity liberalism must be brought to an end" because it has "produced a generation of liberals and progressives narcissistically unaware of conditions outside their self-defined groups." Needless to say, Mr. Lilla advocates abandoning identity politics as a failed project.

But this is a grave mistake. The rise of right-wing identity politics means Americans need to redouble their efforts to understand selfhood and diversity in the modern age. Perhaps no living philosopher has done more to shed light on these questions than the Catholic Canadian Charles Taylor. Mr. Taylor's reputation within contemporary philosophy is formidable. One of the most important contributors to the debates over multiculturalism in the 1990s, he became perhaps the leading thinker in the 2000s on what it means to live in a secular age.

Modern Pluralism

In shortest form, what Americans can learn from Mr. Taylor is the following: The key feature of modern times is pluralism. This means the longstanding view that a secular age is one of increasing unbelief and homogenization of culture around a single set of values is wrong. Instead of homogenization, secularity means an explosion of spiritual and religious options—some traditional, others completely new.

The fact that modernity is primarily characterized by exploding diversity puts the problem of identity squarely at the center of societies like the United States. This means that when Mr. Lilla demands that identity politics "must be brought to an end" he is asking for something that runs against the basic sociological conditions of modernity. Modern people are hyperaware of the diversity of identities and this makes us fragile and insecure. Each of us knows that there are other individuals of intelligence and goodwill who pursue radically different spiritual, political and cultural conceptions of what is good.

This is in sharp contrast to premodern times. For example, in the medieval age, a peasant from Avignon was completely immersed in the horizon of his traditional world. It would have been difficult if not impossible for him to imagine his identity being radically called into jeopardy. It might even have appeared to him to be secured from time immemorial. But we moderns suffer from a very specific anxiety: We sense the radical contingency of our identities as cultural, religious, ethical and spiritual options. We sense that our identities are fragile and expressed not from time immemorial but within a bounded period of historical time. For this reason, we recognize that our identities can either succeed or fail to achieve political legitimacy and social acceptance. There is even the possibility that our identities will be eradicated.

This is what drives humans toward a very modern and heated political project: recognition. Indeed, the drive for identity recognition is perhaps the most distinctly modern political movement. As Mr. Taylor put it in one of the most important essays written on multiculturalism: "[P]eople can suffer real damage ... if the people or society around them mirror back to them a confining or demeaning or contemptible picture of themselves ... Recognition is not just a courtesy we owe people. It is a vital human need."

What Mr. Lilla and Trumpists both equally fail to realize is that identity politics is not simply a self-indulgent preoccupation on the part of liberal elites. Rather, the politics of identity recognition are deeply ingrained into the modern age. Its earliest forms are religious or nationalistic. There are movements to try to restore Christian denominations or confessional identities. There are also mobilizations to achieve the political sovereignty of a particular ethnic or cultural group—Irish, Polish, Puerto Rican, French, Lithuanians and so on. But as modernity has continued to fragment and pluralize, other groups have burst onto the scene and sought recognition as well: second-wave feminists, postcolonialists, the L.G.B.T. coalition, new age philosophies, atheists and many others. Indeed, so universal is the politics of identity that even white ethno-nationalist sites like Breitbart now (falsely) claim: "At the moment, we have identity politics for everyone except white men." (This claim is false because "white" men have had identity politics since the dawn of the modern age through particular cultural and nationalist identities.)

The Dark Side of Identity

The politics of recognition—although it is an almost inescapable feature of modern pluralism—also has a dark side according to Taylor. Insecurity can drive a group to attempt to eliminate diversity as a way out of its sense of fragility amid pluralism. Can the force and authority of the state be used to restore the stability and dominance of a traditional identity? This seems to be the hope to which Breitbart and the more aggressive features of Trumpism appeal. Or, alternatively, perhaps the power of the state can be used as a sanction against traditional moral views in support of newer identity claims. Here parts of the liberal left have arguably overstepped their bounds.

Identity politics is in this way at the very center of the age of Trump. A whole host of writers have been warning us that the culture, faith and habits of white working-class Americans have been demeaned by the urban, liberal elite. J. D. Vance has written a much-discussed memoir, Hillbilly Elegy, about the way this scorn is felt by working-class rural families. "We're more socially isolated than ever," Mr. Vance reports, "and we pass that isolation down to our children." Likewise, many of the Christian conservatives who voted for Donald J. Trump have expressed a deep anxiety about a loss of religious liberty at the hands of those who no longer respect their views.

The backlash against this perceived sneering at white working-class and traditional identities has been undeniably severe. As part of this backlash, other identities have come under attack: Muslims, Hispanics, women, blacks, etc. These groups are increasingly targets of exclusionary rhetoric and reactionary hatred as disaffected white Americans attempt to restore a sense of lost greatness. Hate crimes are up. There is talk among some of Mr. Trump's high-profile supporters of authoritarian measures like keeping a database of "dangerous" religious minorities. The attempt to secure one's sense of identity is linked to some of the most extreme forms of mass violence in the modern world.

So, if identity politics across the political spectrum are an inescapable feature of the fragility introduced by modern pluralism, how does Charles Taylor believe modern people should respond? Should, as Mark Lilla suggests, modern people try to lessen the significance of their identities when it comes to politics? Mr. Taylor suggests a different approach. Basically, debates in society need to be about what constitutes a reasonable amount of pluralism. From this perspective, the big trap American politics has fallen into in recent decades is attempting to canonize particular ethical or moral views through the state (for example, the heated battle over traditional versus gay marriage, or the similar one going on over bathrooms). American politics has been playing a dangerous game, where identities on all sides feel existentially menaced by each new election. Under this analysis, Trumpism is simply the most extreme expression of this anxiety to date.

Instead of terrorizing each other with control of the state every four years, Americans might spend more time finding ways to accommodate a diversity of identities across the political spectrum. The federal government would have a role to play in securing certain rights, but local governments would also allow for different communities to live out their diverse ethics. Rather than trying to create a national moral monoculture through the courts (which misunderstands the meaning of our secular age) Mr. Taylor's brand of multiculturalism seeks to protect a diversity of religious and spiritual options.

All this implies a rather surprising way of looking at how democracies work well in the modern age. Contrary to the view that agreement around human rights is achieved by homogenizing toward a single dominant ethic ("Judeo-Christianity" for conservatives, or "secular progressivism" for liberals, or some version of Enlightenment liberalism for Mr. Lilla), consensus is achieved by allowing for creative re-immersion in particular traditions. We urgently need to reassess what we understand by being "modern" people. Among other things, across the political spectrum we need to become far more comfortable with the cultural and philosophical role of traditions and pluralism. To be an advocate of modern, secular societies, then, means to embrace a pluralism that includes both the traditional identities of the white working class and Muslims, of evangelicals and the L.G.B.T. coalition.

In a recent feature in *The New Yorker*, Mr. Taylor was quoted as saying that dialogue with opponents in the age of Trump is deeply in need of three simple, humble steps: First, "try to listen"; second, "find out what's troubling" your opponent; and third, "stop condemning." In this, Mr. Taylor's Catholic-informed ethic is very close to that of the current pope, who has repeatedly advised Christians that they need to develop "in a special way, the capacity to dialogue and encounter." In other words, contra Mr. Lilla, American society is going to have to become much more comfortable with the deep diversity of identity politics across the entire spectrum of society if it is to fare any better in the coming year than it did in 2016.

EVALUATING THE AUTHOR'S ARGUMENTS:

In this viewpoint, Jason Blakely suggests people should work toward accepting diversity across society and politics. How do his views contrast those in the previous viewpoint? How can people decide when it is time to argue and complain, versus when it is time to accept? What are the advantages and dangers of each behavior?

Intersectionality Is Dividing the LGBTQ Community

Gabriel Arana

In the following excerpted viewpoint, Gabriel Arana argues that some people feel that a focus on intersectionality is dividing the LGBTQ movement, even being used to silence or erase white men in the movement. White gay men may drop out of activism because their primary goals, such as marriage equality, have been achieved. Or they may feel forced out of the movement by people who do not respect their voices. On the other hand, some white gay men feel that their own experience with prejudice makes them more sympathetic to others. Meanwhile, people with multiple disadvantages may want the LGBTQ movement to fight for rights not traditionally associated with the group. These opposing views have led to anger and frustration within the LGBTQ movement. Arana is a contributing editor at The American Prospect and a contributing writer at Salon.

"To those experiencing oppression on several fronts — those at the intersections — the sensibilities of gay white cisgender men seem beside the point."

AS YOU READ, CONSIDER THE FOLLOWING QUESTIONS:

1. How can some members of a disadvantaged group still have privileges, according to this article?
2. Why would some LGBTQ+ activists relax after achieving marriage equality, while others don't see that as so important?
3. Does experiencing only one form of disadvantage make people more or less sensitive to the plight of others?

[...]

For its advocates, intersectionality is a way of centering those who've been historically at the margins of the LGBTQ+ community, whose interests were little served by the arrival of marriage equality.

"Sexism and racism are not just additive, but multiplicative," said Jillian Weiss, executive director of the Transgender Legal Defense & Education Fund. Weiss said that in order to liberate all members of the LGBTQ+ community, it is necessary to elevate those with the least privilege. "Intersectionality is absolutely crucial to our movement—it's not just one thing at a time that we need to fight."

An activist, poet, and grad student at the University of California, Berkeley, Alan Pelaez knows this firsthand.

"The way I navigate the world as an undocumented immigrant is different, as a black queer body is different, [but] I experience these identities simultaneously," said Pelaez, who has urged the LGBTQ+ movement to adopt an intersectional approach to advocacy. "Intersectionality is asking what kinds of privleges some LGBTQ community members have and who gets denied them."

But as dustups caused by groups like No Justice, No Pride show—as well as other developments, like the addition of a brown stripe to Philadelphia's LGBTQ pride flag; and scuffles over the inclusion of Israeli flags at demonstrations—that not everyone is happy with the LGBTQ+ movement's focus on intersectionality, which has foregrounded discussions of privilege, police brutality, sexism, racism, and anti-trans violence.

What message were these Black Lives Matter protesters sending when they interrupted a Pride parade?

Some gay white cisgender men are starting to tune out.

"You have gay white men who are no longer involved in activism or community work because they just get shouted down by minority activists who want to racialize everything," said Jamie Kirchick, a right-leaning journalist and visiting fellow at the Brookings Institution. In a piece in *Tablet* magazine last year titled "How Intersectionality Makes You Stupid," Kirchick took aim at the National LGBTQ+ Task Force, which canceled and then uncanceled a Shabbat reception at its annual Creating Change conference in response to critics of Israel.

"White gay man has become an epithet," he added.

While the academic definition of intersectionality may be narrow, its meaning has broadened as its usage has spread across various social justice movements. Not only is it used as shorthand to talk about work between coalitions, it has also come to embody the idea that, as with the experience of identity, the sources of oppression—sexism, homophobia, transphobia, racism—are interconnected. For the more radical, the ultimate oppressor is capitalism.

"I think what [the focus on intersectionality] does is bring everyone to rally around our victimhood, and that, fundamentally, is negative," said Jimmy LaSalvia, now a political independent who co-founded gay Republican group the Log Cabin Republicans. "A bigger, more unifying message will resonate with more and more of Americans as we grow tired of the us-versus-them confrontation-style politics of the last couple of decades."

Kirchick said intersectionality has made the work of some LGBTQ+ organizations incoherent, citing groups like Gays Against Guns, which sprung up after the Pulse massacre in Orlando last year.

"You can support gun control, but I don't see what that has to do with being gay," Kirchick said. "And the notion that gay-rights groups should be weighing in at all on [the] abortion issue is preposterous."

Erasing Gay White Cisgender Men?

But even some progressive gay white men say they feel alienated from a movement they see becoming more radical, particularly online, where the tenor of conversation is often uncivil. Writing in *The Nation* in 2014, *New York Times* columnist Michelle Goldberg noted a similar dynamic emerging online between older feminists and younger ones who consider themselves intersectionalists.

One left-leaning political activist and writer, who asked for anonymity for fear of reprisal, said he often gets shouted down on social media by intersectionalists decrying his "white privilege" and minimizing both his struggles and contributions to the movement. This includes downplaying the role of gay men in the 1969 Stonewall riots that kicked off the modern-day LGBTQ-rights era.

"People literally say that gay white men have done nothing for the movement for the last 50 years," he said. "They're not trying to make the movement intersectional; they're trying to erase other participants who came before them."

"A lot of people are staying on the sidelines just because of the intensity of the expected attacks," said Walter K. Olson, a fellow at libertarian think tank the Cato Institute. "For a lot of people—even people who support [intersectionality] but may have a sticking point —they just feel they had better stay out of the conversation."

But Olson, who is gay and married, added that the internal conflict the LGBTQ+ movement is currently experiencing—and the drop-off in participation from those at the top—was to be expected after marriage equality.

"Movements change after they win," Olson said. "After victory, you will naturally lose a lot of your momentum."

Olson provided himself as an example. A gay white married man, he said he "showed up for marriage and looked at issues that followed and stepped back out." While he supports trans rights, he said he feels the battle is no longer his.

Another "Movement of Movements"

Older activists also believe that critiques of the LGBTQ+ movement's inclusivity overlook past progress. Richard Rosendall, a columnist for the *Washington Blade* and a decades-long activist, said the LGBTQ+ movement in Washington, D.C., has always been allied with the racial-justice groups, given the city's racial diversity. During the marriage fight, he worked with black faith leaders who supported gay marriage. The NAACP endorsed marriage equality at the time, which suggests that LGBTQ+ groups have often worked with other rights organizations to achieve its goals.

"To pretend there has been no progress on [race within the LGBTQ+ community] disincentivizes allyship," Rosendall said.

While Rosendall generally supports intersectional approaches to activism, he penned a column criticizing No Justice, No Pride for interrupting D.C. Pride. He said protesting police presence at Pride overlooks decades of work spent improving relations between the D.C. LGBTQ+ community and the police force; the department even has an LGBTQ+ liaison and is considered a model for inclusion.

"There's a risk of behaving in a totalitarian mindset," he said.

Stein, the SF State historian, noted that the current debate within the LGBTQ+ movement over issues of inclusion—and what "justice for all" means—is reminiscent of what academics call the "movement of movements" in the late 1960s and early 1970s. United by the Vietnam War, it was an "incredible era of dialogue" between social-justice groups of starkly different stripes.

The Gay Liberation Front marched with the Black Panthers and participated in antiwar demonstrations. "Homophiles," as they called themselves back then, took on issues like police reform at a time when law enforcement routinely entrapped gay men in stings. The movement was not only far more decentralized than today, when several large LGBTQ+ advocacy organizations with lots of money generally set the agenda; it was stacked with critics of capitalism, including communists like Harry Hay, who co-founded early homophile organization the Mattachine Society. In 1989, the first gay-pride march through Washington, D.C., featured a conference that tried to encourage coalitions between different racial groups; it was endorsed by the National Organization for Women and the National Coalition of Black Lesbians and Gays.

To call the "movement of movements" intersectional would be an anachronism, but the banding together of different causes produced similarly contentious debates about who had power, whose issues should take precedence, and which coalitions made sense. Now, with President Donald Trump in the White House, intersectionalists are posing similar questions.

"This Is Not a Polite Thing"

To those experiencing oppression on several fronts—those at the intersections—the sensibilities of gay white cisgender men seem beside the point.

"I come from a place of anger—particularly on social media, where people who are oppressed talk about their embodied knowledge—but my anger is rooted in the fact that my human limits have been met," said activist Pelaez, adding that the arrival of marriage equality did little to help his legal status. "Anger is generative and a source of empowerment. Only when we are angry can we do something to address what makes us angry."

Lourdes Hunter, a black trans woman and the executive director of the TransWomen of Color Collective, put it more starkly.

"When black trans women are murdered in the street, it doesn't happen in a polite manner," said Hunter, an academic who has worked as an organizer for 25 years. Indeed, trans women of color are more frequently the victims of violence than any other group under the LGBTQ umbrella.

"This is not a polite thing," Hunter said. "When someone has their foot on your neck, you don't tap them and say, 'Excuse me.'"

With Trump in office, the most marginalized members of the LGBTQ community feel that the need to speak out against threats forcefully is more critical than the need to engage in "respectability politics."

"There are people who are undocumented, with disabilities, impacted by state-sanctioned violence in ways cisgender white queer people are not," Hunter said. "With intersectionality, we're talking about centering those voices that have been erased by cisgender white queers."

"Sometimes the framework for the liberation of one group clashes with another," Pelaez added, citing the rhetoric around immigration as an example. Public sympathy centers around Dreamers—undocumented Americans brought to the US as children—and those who have committed no crimes. Linking citizenship with lack of criminality undermines the racial-justice movement's critique of the way certain groups are presumed criminal and overpoliced.

"We use narratives about immigrants that implicate blacks," he said. "I'm not going to be liberated because I am both black and an immigrant."

The calls for politeness strike Darnell Moore, a writer and organizer with Black Lives Matter who identifies as queer and black, as "disingenuous." He noted that AIDS activism in the 1980s and 1990s—in which gay men and their allies chained themselves to government buildings and performed die-ins on the streets of major cities—was hardly polite.

"So the only people who are allowed to be disruptive are white cisgender men?" said Moore, who called on LGBTQ organizations to endorse Black Lives Matter on HuffPost.

Our Allies, Our Selves

Not all gay white cisgender men see the LGBTQ+ movement's intersectional turn in a negative light. Gay Pennsylvania Rep. Brian Sims said his experience as a gay white cisgender man—and the discrimination he has faced on account of his sexual orientation—has made him more sympathetic to the plight of members of the community who are more disenfranchised than he is.

"I don't think I've ever seen it as victimhood," said Sims, who supported the addition of a brown stripe to Philadelphia's pride flag. "We talk about the Obama years as a heyday for the gay movement. That's not true for hundreds of thousands of LGBT people. It didn't change the circumstances of trans women of color."

Sims said it seemed obvious to him that sexism, racism, transphobia, ableism, and homophobia come from the same place, and said that the far-right politics of the Trump administration have made intersectionality all the more important.

"If sharing a common enemy brings us together, the best thing that comes from this Dumpster fire of a presidency is that we are all learning that we can and should work together," he said. "It doesn't water down the [experience of gay white cisgender men] to hear about others' struggles. It informs you to make better decisions."

[...]

It remains to be seen how intersectionality within the LGBTQ+ community will play out, whether it will be seen, decades from now, as sparking the kind of vital progress Stonewall or AIDS activism did. Or will it come to be understood as a force that fragmented queer politics and alienated gay white cisgender men, long-considered that movement's most powerful group? In large part, the answer depends on whether those with more power will step aside and let those with less speak and be heard, and whether they feel they are sharing power rather than losing it.

EVALUATING THE AUTHOR'S ARGUMENTS:

Viewpoint author Gabriel Arana discusses concerns that intersectionality is being used to silence some people in the LGBTQ+ movement. Compare this to viewpoint 5 in Chapter 1, where the author suggests that people with more privilege should speak less and listen more. Does everyone deserve an equal voice in an activist movement, regardless of the number of disadvantages he or she has? Why or why not?

We All Can Fight Together for Freedom

"All forms of social life are already coded by class, race, gender and disability, so there are no forms of politics or struggle that exist outside these structures of social power."

Sofa Gradin

In the following viewpoint, Sofa Gradin argues that, though people are individuals and that perspective should be respected, everyone on the left is fighting the same struggle. The author suggests that each side can learn from the other to build unity. She notes that class struggle is connected to questions of identity; race, gender, and disability affect one's class, or place in society. In her view the real question is how to integrate intersectionality into the class struggle. She suggests that traditional liberal politics attempt to add minorities into the existing structure. Intersectionality, on the other hand, attempts to expand and change that structure to understand and value diversity. Gradin teaches Politics at Kings College London.

AS YOU READ, CONSIDER THE FOLLOWING QUESTIONS:

1. What are goals of liberalism, as described in this article?
2. Why is it impossible for individuals to enjoy absolute freedom and autonomy?
3. In the author's view, why is an identity more than an individual freedom?

"Is there really a crisis around identity politics on the left?" by Sofa Gradin, This article was originally published in the independent online magazine opendemocracy.net, June 12, 2017. Reprinted by permission.

Social codes such as race, gender, and class are present from the beginning of our lives. Instead of letting that divide us, can we find a way to use it to our advantage?

Two recent encounters with fellow lefties have got me thinking.

One day I'm at a Leninist meeting talking to a Marxist dude who's bemoaning the increased popularity of "identity politics" within the left, because it distracts from the "real struggle" of ending material exploitation.

And the next day I'm in the basement of a queer bar watching a drag artist shouting to rapturous applause that being "non-binary" means to be free to be whatever you want to be—celebrating personal freedom as a key element of social transformation.

Both of these people belong to and identify with the left, but they seem to represent contradictory positions on a question that's consuming an awful lot of our energies these days: how to respond to the multifaceted realities of oppression and liberation.

As a queer non-binary Marxist, I can see where both positions are coming from. On the one hand, I want everyone on the left to understand that we're all fighting the same struggle—that it's people's material wellbeing that matters in the end. On the other hand, everyone within the Left isn't the same—there are many identities, cultures, sexualities and personal expressions that need to be respected.

What are we supposed to do with these tensions? How should the left respond?

Social Codes

Conventional wisdom says "take one side or the other," but that cements internal divisions still further just when we need more unity. It's better to recognise that this split itself is artificial, and that both positions can learn from the other. Let me explain.

Since the 1970s the left has grappled with its own exclusion of marginalised people. Women, people of colour, disabled folks, queers and others have drawn attention to the assumptions and behaviours that have sidelined their needs and interests. In a ground breaking public statement issued in 1977, the Boston-based Black feminist group Combahee River Collective highlighted their need to "develop a politics that was anti-racist, unlike those of white women, and anti-sexist, unlike those of Black and white men."

Since then, many groups and individuals have developed a radical "intersectional" critique which argues that sexism, racism and other forms of oppression in mainstream society are often reproduced within the left. As legal scholar Kimberlé Crenshaw pointed out in the 1980s, struggles in aid of equality for vulnerable people have often failed to recognise that oppression works along several axes at once. There has been an implicit assumption on much of the left that the working class is white, male, non-disabled and straight, so the obstacles faced by the majority are ignored.

But now, many on the left are sceptical of this intersectional discourse, arguing that an "incessant" focus on personal characteristics distracts from the common struggle against capitalism—that intersectional politics has become, as Marxist commentator Asad Haider puts it "not about a social structure, but [about] the recognition of an individual or a particular group's identity."

Haider continues:

> *Now in an organizing meeting, any discussion that takes place between a white person and a person of color will be tense and guarded, because at any time the white person may be accused of white privilege, and thus denounced for bringing irreconcilable political interests into the group. That is a very different kind of politics, and not one that tends to result in open strategic discussions, building trust between activists, or effectively broadening towards a mass movement.*

As these tensions intensify, it's very important to clear something up: radical queerness and anti-racism are not forms of identity politics; and class struggle is not free from questions of identity. All forms of social life are already coded by class, race, gender and disability, so there are no forms of politics or struggle that exist outside these structures of social power. The claim that intersectional critiques distract from the "real struggle" or are divisive is based on a fundamental misunderstanding of both intersectionality and socialism: the question is not whether the two can be integrated, but how.

These misconceptions are, however, understandable, in part because intersectional critiques have arisen at the same time as a parallel liberal discourse in mainstream society which is about identity politics. This liberal discourse demands the recognition of non-dominant identities in society: that a Black person can be president; that people with disabilities can be entrepreneurs; that women can be corporate CEOs; and that gay people can get married. These demands, which seem obviously desirable and therefore politically neutral, are in fact the product of a particular political ideology, namely liberalism.

At the time of its initial development in early modern Europe, liberalism was a new and radical philosophy that broke away from the traditional feudal belief in a highly regulated social order based on monarchy and serfdom. Instead it emphasised the importance of individual freedom and non-interference by the state or by other people in the private sphere. Every person has the right to behave as they see fit unless they actively cause harm to someone else.

In response to older beliefs that homosexuality cannot be respectable, for example, or that people of colour are "naturally" different from white people, the assertion that marginalised groups are just as human and important as dominant groups is certainly a form of progress. But what liberalism fails to understand is that it isn't possible to create a just and free society on the basis of these principles. As many on the left have pointed out (including Marx himself), human beings are deeply social creatures who depend on and co-create each other, so no individual can enjoy absolute freedom and autonomy.

The Personal Becomes the Political

Liberals believe that the decisions we make about our lives are personal—that where we work, what we say and how we spend our money, dress and behave is nobody's business but our own. However, once we realise that people are deeply interconnected these allegedly personal decisions become public and political. Our jobs, for example, are connected to a broader economy that involves a myriad of other workers, consumers and producers.

As a result of these interconnections, certain repeated patterns have emerged through the evolution of Western society that have penetrated deep into our personal lives and personalities. For example, British women have not randomly chosen to do two thirds more housework than men. Black women working in white collar jobs are not constantly mistaken for office cleaners by pure chance. And two women per week are not just accidentally killed by men in cases of domestic violence. As these examples show, expressions of power that shape public life also make their way into private thought and action, and vice-versa.

Intersectional critiques may look similar to liberal identity politics on the surface, but at their core they are not concerned with assimilating marginalised groups into existing mainstream institutions, language and positions. Rather, the goal is to rethink and reconstruct those institutions altogether. And that effort starts by examining how the structures of power that create and regulate race, class, gender, disabiity and sexuality play out in our own lives and in our own organising, as well as in society more broadly.

Hence, instead of encouraging a disabled woman to dominate a panel discussion just as assertively as any non-disabled man, we can organise participatory workshops and train ourselves on how to take part in inclusive discussions. We can rethink our demands and strategies; redesign our posters and websites; change the language we use and our demeanour in meetings and at home; and resist the nation-state by creating more deeply-democratic and participatory forms of governance. In these ways we don't merely add minorities to existing political practices and structures as liberal identity politics aims to do—we transform them around a much deeper understanding of diversity.

By the same token, the claim that non-binary queerness is solely an expression of individual freedom is based on a liberal misunderstanding. For me, being queer is not just a private preference, it's about how I behave, know, talk, organise, work and live. Being queer is a necessary response to structural oppression; a vehicle to confront and resist the ways in which capitalism, racism and patriarchy seep into the most intimate aspects of my life. Queerness is not freedom from social interference, it's the opposite—an active and responsible engagement with the structures of social power.

Therefore, rather than bemoaning the increased popularity of identity politics we should rethink our forms of organising, core questions and priorities. We must let go of the notion that the working class—or the ruling class—are homogenous. To include the concerns of many women, people of colour, queers and disabled people we must organise in the home, in community centres and night clubs, with accessible toilets and hearing loops, for alternatives to racist and violent policing, against gender norms and borders, and with sensitivity, emotion and attention to the needs and voices of specific groups as well as the goals that unite us.

EVALUATING THE AUTHOR'S ARGUMENTS:

In this viewpoint, Sofa Gradin tries to reconcile intersectionality with the goal of working toward a common struggle. Do you think she succeeds? Using examples from her viewpoint, why or why not?

Chapter 3

Where Should We Go with Identity Politics?

How can a country as large and diverse as America ensure all voices are heard?

Sometimes You Should Just Listen

"When I first started trying to understand this intersectional world of online activism, I quickly learned to listen more and say less."

Katelyn Giel

In the following viewpoint, Katelyn Giel describes her experience at a national women's march. She then compares white women's treatment of women of color to men's treatment of women. The more powerful group may tell the oppressed group to ignore race or gender in order to build unity "for the greater good." Also, the more privileged group may often be defensive. People may deny accusations and make excuses rather than acknowledge their privilege. The author recommends listening to other viewpoints and trying to find ways to work together and help other groups. Giel has written for several publications, including *Bottle Magazine*, a site "written by women for everyone about everything."

AS YOU READ, CONSIDER THE FOLLOWING QUESTIONS:

1. What is the value of listening when someone complains about your behavior as an activist, according to the author?
2. Why might women of color accuse white women of being unsympathetic or untrustworthy?
3. What does the author mean by "white nonsense"?

"On White Nonsense: An Intersectionality Primer," by Katelyn Giel, *Bottle Magazine*, January 24, 2017. Reprinted by permission.

The 2017 Women's March was criticized for its failure to include women other than white, middle-class women in a meaningful way.

This week, I had the incredible privilege of marching on the National Mall in D.C. with hundreds of thousands of my sisters in what turned out to be a cathartic, empowering, exhilarating day. We marched so our voices would be heard and because too often we are spoken over and spoken for. We marched for reproductive healthcare, refugees, gun control, prison reform, immigration reform, anti-poverty policy, and dozens of other critical, life-or-death policies that simply can't wait any longer.

Many men said this march wouldn't change anything—that we were wasting our time. They said we should suck it up and respect the president. They said we should put our concerns aside for the sake of unity. They said #NotAllMen.

And we said hell no. We told them to take a step into our shoes, to have some empathy. We told them that we have life experiences that they couldn't possibly understand, that they should trust women, and that we won't wait any longer. So we marched.

I marched with elderly women who paved the way for me and little girls for whom I will hopefully help pave their way. I marched with mothers shaken out of their apathy for fear of their daughters and young women who gathered the courage to march even though their parents wouldn't understand. I marched with all kinds of women from all walks of life; I marched with trans women and immigrant women and Black women and brown women and Native women and disabled women and LGB women and even lots of men. But mostly, I marched with lots and lots of white women.

One quiet, older Black woman held a sign that read "Stop the White Nonsense." I marched near her for a few moments and heard two middle-aged white women tell her that it's offensive to reduce everything white people say to nonsense and that nonsense doesn't have a color.

eyeroll

What Is Intersectional Feminism?
Let's take a step back. I know lots of the women in my life have begun approaching activism for the first time in the aftermath of the election, and I know that the initial approach can be really overwhelming and intimidating. It's jarring when the framework with which you were conditioned to view the world fractures and you have to reevaluate the very lens that lets you see. So I don't expect those women to already know this. But I do expect them to learn.

So let's talk about intersectional feminism, how white women do to women of color what men do to us, and ending white nonsense.

For those unfamiliar, intersectionality is the idea that we all have multiple identities that frame how we interact with the world. For example, I'm a woman and I'm young and I'm white and I'm fat and I have anxiety and I'm cisgender (meaning I identify with the gender I was assigned at birth) and I'm straight and I come from a middle class family. Some of my identities have given me privilege (like being white) and some have placed me in a position of oppression (like being a woman). But when I interact with the world, I interact with it as my whole self, at the intersection of all my identities. So, I don't leave my whiteness at the door when I experience things as a woman, and I'm still a woman when I'm experiencing white privilege.

What this means is that we all experience womanhood differently. I experience it as a straight, cis, middle-class white woman. Some of my sisters experience it as Black women or immigrant women or trans women or poor women or some combination of those things. When I experience workplace sexual harassment or am catcalled or experience being on the wrong side of the wage gap or am spoken over, I am always cloaked in my whiteness. It's inherent that my understanding of womanhood is only an understanding of white, straight, cis, middle-class womanhood.

So when a Native woman explains the pain and marginalization she felt marching among lots of white women, I listen because I have no idea what it is to interact with the world as a Native woman. Or when Black Lives Matter activists wonder why it's so damn hard to get white ladies to BLM protests, why they're just now willing to take to the streets, I listen and I try to understand and I make a plan to figure out how I can help. Or when our trans sisters talk about the pain they felt seeing signs at the march that centered womanhood entirely around having a uterus, I listen, try to empathize with their pain and to think about how I can best phrase my activism. Or when a non-white protester holds up a sign that says "White Women Voted for Trump," I don't yell back, "Not all white women!" I listen and I hear her point and I wonder how I can talk to my white friends about voting. Or when social media activists complain that white allies can't be trusted, I listen, wonder what it would feel like to feel like nobody is on your side and commit to trying to be a better ally. Or when a Black woman posts in a comment thread that white women should just shut up and listen for once, I do. I listen and I don't speak or comment.

The Importance of Self-Examination

When I first started trying to understand this intersectional world of online activism, I quickly learned to listen more and say less. My voice is very often not the most interesting one in the room (or the comment thread), and I almost always have the least number of identities that would make me marginalized or oppressed and a whole lot more privilege than those around me. Sometimes I ask questions, but whenever possible, I ask them of white folks more woke than I am—or of Google—because marginalized folks are emotionally exhausted and do not owe us their time or labor. Before I say or do anything, I try to understand how a Black woman or a trans woman or any other woman would perceive my words and what it would feel like to experience them in her shoes.

It's important to remember that when someone is talking about white people or white women, they might not be talking about you. When someone says "White people are racist!" or "White progressives don't actually do anything for us!" take a breath first. If it's not about you, it's not about you. Move on.

If it is about you, do some serious introspection. Interrogate your own biases and behaviors to understand why it brought your defenses up so quickly. Your privilege—being white—is not an evil thing or a condemnation of your character. It doesn't mean you've never worked or felt pain. It's inherent to your identity and, if you do the work of understanding it and restructuring your worldview, it might even be a tool you can use to help your more marginalized sisters down the road.

Remember how it felt when men said this march wouldn't change anything, that we were wasting our time? When they said we should suck it up and respect the president? That we should put our concerns aside for the sake of unity? #NotAllMen? That exasperation we feel when they just don't get it because they're limiting themselves to their own experience? In those moments, they denied the experience that we have of interacting with the world as women. They didn't trust us or defer to us.

That's how women of color feel when we tell them to stop bringing race into things and focus on the fact that we're all women. When we say things like "Not all white women voted for Trump!" not only are we derailing the conversation, but we're dismissing the reality that they experience—and the reality that a majority of white women did. Trust and defer to women of color, because they know what it's like to exist at the intersection of their identities better than we ever will. Just as we ask men to step outside of themselves and empathize with the experience of interacting with the world while female, we must step outside of yourselves and empathize with the reality of interacting with the world as a woman of color.

When they say "Stop the white nonsense!" ask yourself who and what they're talking about. 53% of white women just voted for Trump and a huge chunk of the rest of us—the Hillary and Jill voters—have refused to show up for intersectional feminist causes in that past.

If it's not about you, it's not about you. But what can you do to ease that pain? What cause can you take up or whose mind can you change? White nonsense is not the collective actions of all white people being categorically reduced to nonsense. It is the persistent presence of white people who dismiss the experiences of people of color, betray their causes, and perpetuate racism both passively and actively. White nonsense is the dangerous election of Trump by white women who just weren't really feelin' Hillary 'cause she felt kinda cold and the rise of #AllLivesMatter and the refusal of white feminists to recognize the experiences of women of color as a cross that the collective sisterhood should bear. So what can you do about those things?

Marginalized folks are done waiting. We made Black suffragettes march in the back in 1913 because we figured "One thing at a time! Let's make our cause easy and palatable!" and then many of them didn't actually have access to the vote until 50 years later. No more. We won't go back. We're not sweeping our differences under the rug. We're embracing them and we're fighting for all of them. It's time for white feminists to march in the back, supporting and prioritizing their more marginalized sisters.

It is easy to walk away from this at first because you don't understand and because the learning curve is steep. It is harder to swallow your pride, pick up bell hooks' collected works, sit down with a friend at a coffee shop, and really dig into what your privilege means and how you should alter your activism to fight for all your sisters.

But if I'm being honest, if your feminism isn't intersectional, it's trash. If your feminism doesn't center the most marginalized of your sisters, then what's the point? Lower your defenses, stop centering your own emotions in these conversations, realize the immense privilege you have, and listen, listen, listen.

Let's end white nonsense, shall we?

EVALUATING THE AUTHOR'S ARGUMENTS:

Viewpoint author Katelyn Giel writes that she learned to listen more and say less in the world of activism. Does her response seem rational? At what point should one speak rather than listen? Should people who face more oppression speak more often?

Don't Talk About Race Without Discussing Class

"Discussing race without including class analysis is like watching a bird fly without looking at the sky: it's possible, but it misses the larger context."

Rhonda Soto

In the following viewpoint, Rhonda Soto argues that concepts of class are not discussed in America as much as they should be. Instead, the focus is often singly on race. This can lead to reinforcement of negative stereotypes, such as the assumption that people of color are from low-income families and white students are not. These stereotypes can make it hard for people who don't fit them to succeed. The author claims that educational institutions should be more aware of how class affects students. They can then make changes to help students of all backgrounds succeed. Soto is the coordinator of the Race/Class Intersections program at Class Action, a nonprofit that aims to end classism.

AS YOU READ, CONSIDER THE FOLLOWING QUESTIONS:
1. What is the problem with confusing race and class, according to the author?
2. Why are low-income students often poorly prepared for college success?
3. What is cultural capital and why is it important, according to the viewpoint?

Race and class are too often conflated in debates about struggling groups in the United States. It is important to remember that race and class are two distinct categorizations.

Discussing race without including class analysis is like watching a bird fly without looking at the sky: it's possible, but it misses the larger context. Intersections of race and class are complicated and personal, and they need to be acknowledged. Yet in the United States, so little talk about class occurs that great confusion surrounds these intersections. As the coordinator of the Race/Class Intersections program at the nonprofit Class Action (www.classism.org), I have heard from many people who say our conversation is the first time they have publicly discussed the intersection of race and class. They search for the right words to express the complicated relationship between these categories, and find that it defies existing frameworks.

Much of Class Action's work takes place at institutions of higher education. We work with professional and administrative staff, students, and community members to identify and dismantle class barriers and biases, and to build opportunities for cross-class alliances. Class remains largely invisible on college campuses, as most institutions do not include class in their campus dialogues, diversity training, or curricular offerings. The lack of discussion about class has led to confusion about the race/class intersection, with race sometimes becoming a stand-in for class. This is problematic not only for the many first-generation college students who are people of color, but also for students whose race- and class-based identities do not intersect in stereotypical ways.

Complicated Junctures

When race becomes a stand-in for class, it creates conflict for students of color who are presumed to be from low-income families and for white students who are presumed not to be. We hear the terms "working-class whites" and "middle-class blacks," but not the terms "middle-class whites" or "working-class blacks." But it is unnecessary to name what is normative. Thus our discussions about "the working class" and "people of color" make working-class white students and middle-class students of color invisible, which can be devastating to these students. At the same time, our language suggests indifference to working-class people of color, who are accepted as the norm. In order to serve the full range of students on our campuses, we must deal with issues of racism and issues of classism, and we must understand how they intersect.

Research confirms ever-widening disparities in educational achievement and enrollment among Latinas/os, African Americans, and low-income students, as compared to their white middle- and upper-class peers (Kelly 2005). Because

school resources are tied to local revenues, students from low-income communities, who are disproportionately people of color, are more likely to have inexperienced teachers, limited resources, and little access to role models or mentors (Annie E. Casey Foundation 2008). They enter college without adequate preparation for success, and their transition to higher education is often difficult. Moreover, families with limited income may not be able to spare their hardworking college-age children, who could contribute financially rather than plunge the family into debt with education loans.

The challenges related to resources are often compounded by the psychological pressures low-income students, particularly low-income students of color, face. College definitely has a "class culture," and it isn't the culture of working-class or lower-income students. Research tells us that college is a middle-class experience and that many low-income students feel pressured to assimilate (DiMaria 2006). Race and ethnicity may deepen these students' feelings of isolation, especially if they come from families whose culture and language differs from that of majority students. Perception and judgments of faculty and peers have an impact as well. Because affirmative action is a hot-button issue, students of color may find themselves prejudged by their peers and professors, even as the numbers of (typically white) legacy admissions exceed the number of affirmative action admissions.

The presence or absence of cultural, social, and academic capital can also have a profound impact on students. Pierre Bourdieu describes cultural capital, or what you know, as the forms of knowledge, skill, education, and other advantages a person has that confer higher status (1986). Knowing the rules of etiquette (such as which fork to use) or understanding references to theater are examples of cultural capital. Social capital, or who you know, refers to resources based on group membership, relationships, or networks of influence and support (Bourdieu 1986). To these Will Barratt adds the concept of academic capital, which students begin to attain in the home (2007). Second-generation students come to college with accumulated academic capital, which they apply to gain more through excellent grades, honors and awards, and participation in academic clubs. Students of color and lower-income students may have significant cultural or social capital within their own communities, but the dominant academic culture might not recognize or appreciate these forms of capital.

Supporting Students

If educational institutions are to embrace all of their students and staff, they must address the impact of race and class on the experiences and successes of students. Acknowledging the existence of class on campus is an important first step. Some elite colleges, recognizing that few students from lower-income families are attending their schools, have recently increased financial aid to recruit high-achieving students from low-income families. But getting poor and working-class students through the door is only the beginning. Institutions need to take additional steps (including revising the curricula, providing support services, and reducing cultural barriers, as detailed in the sidebar) to provide adequate support so students can succeed and thrive.

EVALUATING THE AUTHOR'S ARGUMENTS:

In this viewpoint, Rhonda Soto says that most Americans do not discuss the intersection of race and class. Have you ever talked or thought about that intersection before? Do you think it is important for people to do so?

Financial Inequality Exists in Every Racial Group

Eric London

"American society is increasingly polarized— not between races, but between classes."

In the following viewpoint, Eric London argues that financial inequality exists for every racial group. Regardless of race, the wealthiest people get wealthier while the poor stay poor. Meanwhile the groups in the middle have lost substantial wealth. London claims that the true division in America is by economic classes, not race. He suggests that upper-class people of color are intentionally ignoring this in order to improve their own lives. The answer, he says, is to work for social equality by linking all workers through socialism. London is a writer for The World Socialist Web Site.

AS YOU READ, CONSIDER THE FOLLOWING QUESTIONS:

1. What has happened to the division of wealth in the United States, according to the viewpoint?
2. What is the division of wealth among racial minority groups?
3. What does the author believe should unite workers of all races?

In recent years, wealth has increased for the richest in each racial group, making the income inequality divide more about class than race.

A September 2017 report published by the Federal Reserve shows that social inequality in the US has grown to record levels over the last decade. From 2004 to 2016, the wealth of the bottom 90 percent of the population drastically declined while the top 1 percent saw a sharp increase.

The data also show that the growth in social inequality is most acute within racial minorities. Over the course of the last 10 years, affluent African-Americans and Latinos have seen their wealth skyrocket at the expense of the working class of all races.

This large shift of wealth has had a dramatic impact on the social anatomy of the population, placing wind behind the sails of sections of the affluent upper-middle class whose racialist political outlook has come to play a dominant role in bourgeois politics.

Matt Bruenig of the People's Policy Project analyzed data from the Federal Reserve report and showed the extreme degree of inequality within racial minority groups.

Among both African-American and Latino populations, roughly 65 percent own zero percent of the total wealth owned by their respective racial groups. The richest 10 percent of African-Americans own 75.3 percent of all wealth owned by African-Americans; the richest 10 percent of Latinos own 77.9 percent of all Latino wealth; and 74.6 percent of the wealth owned by whites is owned by the top 10 percent of whites.

The level of inequality within racial groups has skyrocketed since the coming to power of Barack Obama. Over the course of his presidency, from 2007 to 2016, the top 1 percent of African-Americans increased its share from 19.4 percent to 40.5 percent. Among Latinos, the top 1 percent increased its share from 30.7 to 44.7. The figure also increased among whites, but less dramatically, from 31.9 to 36.5.

In another dataset, Bruenig shows that during the Obama administration, wealth for the top 1 percent of African-Americans and Latinos skyrocketed, while declining for the bottom 99 percent within those groups.

Bruenig also explains that due to higher levels of poverty among African-Americans and Latinos, only the top 2 percent within each racial group has sufficient wealth to enter the overall top 10 percent among all racial groups. In other words, the years 2007 to 2016 further devastated Latino and black working people while greatly enriching the minority members of the wealthiest 10 percent.

The Federal Reserve data show that the wealth of Latinos in the overall top 10 percent increased by $298,161 from 2007 to 2016, and by $275,414 for African-Americans in this group. The wealth of those whites who comprise the top 10 percent overall also increased under Obama.

Bruenig's analysis also shows that sections of the Latino and African-American working class which had previously been more economically stable—those in the 60th to 95th percentile in their respective groups, and situated in the 40th to 80th percentile overall—were particularly devastated from 2007 to 2016, as compared to the poorer halves of their racial groups who also lost wealth but had less to lose. These sections of the minority working class, which would have had relatively well-paying jobs with benefits in earlier decades, lost between $100,000 and $350,000 over the past decade.

A Polarized Nation

This massive transfer of wealth exposes the sham of Obama's presidency. Hailed by the corporate media and pseudo-left as a "transformative figure" on account of his race, his administration oversaw the bank bailout, the bankruptcy of Detroit, the poisoning of the water in Flint, the deportation of 2.7 million immigrants, the expansion of NSA surveillance and a permanent state of war, and major cuts to social programs, education and food stamps.

The Democratic Party consciously used Obama's skin color to give a political cover to social counterrevolution. The super-rich were primary beneficiaries, but the affluent middle class, including sections of African-Americans and Latinos, were among the greatest beneficiaries of this policy of intensified class exploitation. This created the conditions for the victory of Trump, who benefited from a decline in the vote for the candidate of Wall Street, Hillary Clinton, among all workers, including minority workers.

The Federal Reserve report shows that workers of all racial groups face declining wealth and stagnant incomes, and that growing economic hardship is prevalent across different strata of the working class. In other words, workers of different races and at differing income and wealth levels are objectively being drawn closer together by the impact of the ruling class's social counterrevolutionary policies.

American society is increasingly polarized—not between races, but between classes. In this context, the class basis of the upper-middle class's obsession with racial and identity politics becomes clearer. This is the reactionary political essence of groups like Black Lives Matter, authors like Ta-Nehisi Coates, and academics like Keeyanga-Yamahtta Taylor, who push racial politics to better fleece the working class members of their "own" racial groups, and the working class overall.

Their claims of a unitary "black community" or "Latino community" are fraudulent attempts to hide the immense class divisions that exist within these groups. At the same time, the affluent sections of these racial groups seek to manipulate discontent to advance their own claims to a greater share of wealth and privilege within the top 10 percent.

Identity politics has become a key mechanism through which the next 9 percent situated below the top 1 percent advances its grievances within the political establishment, fighting for "space" in the universities, trade unions, political parties, state apparatus, and corporate media. This layer, which forms a principal social base for the Democratic Party, is generally pro-war and supportive of the right-wing policies that have produced a soaring stock market.

Socialists fight not for a redistribution of wealth within the top 10 percent, but for a complete restructuring of society to abolish social inequality and end the domination of the corporate and financial elite over social and economic life. The social basis for the building of a revolutionary socialist movement lies in the bottom 90 percent, the working class, which will attract the support of the most socially-conscious and humane elements among the next 9 percent.

The social interests of all nationalities, races and social strata of workers are being drawn together by the impact of the social counterrevolutionary policies of the two parties. The task of socialists is to fight to give political expression to this objective process, breaking the barriers of racial chauvinism, linking workers across the world in a common revolutionary fight for social equality and socialism.

EVALUATING THE AUTHOR'S ARGUMENTS:

Viewpoint author Eric London claims that class divisions, not race, have caused social inequality. Compare this viewpoint to the previous one, which discussed the intersection of race and class. How do these viewpoints use or ignore intersectionality? What is the result in their philosophies?

Politics That Ignore Identity Will Fragment Society

"Political leaders should make clear that rights are not a zero-sum game; protecting my rights does not undermine yours."

Boris Dittrich

In the following viewpoint, Boris Dittrich addresses the issue of whether politicians suffer from embracing identity politics. He gives three examples of cases when liberal politicians may have lost elections because they focused on the rights of disadvantaged groups. However, he argues, this is not a reason to ignore diversity. Disadvantaged groups are only demanding equal rights. This should be supported, even if it does not win elections. Dittrich is a former Dutch politician who now leads Human Rights Watch's advocacy efforts on the rights of LGBT people around the world.

AS YOU READ, CONSIDER THE FOLLOWING QUESTIONS:

1. How could a politician be "punished" for supporting the rights of certain disadvantage groups?
2. Why is empathy important to human rights, according to the author?
3. What does the author mean by saying that "rights are not a zero-sum game"?

"Identity Politics Forever," by Boris Dittrich, Advocacy Director, LGBT Program HRW, HERE PUBLISH-ING INC., April 3, 2017. First published in The Advocate. Reprinted by permission.

Actress Laverne Cox is the rare example of a trangender woman with privilege. The truth is, trans women are at greater risk of facing discrimination, being unemployed, and becoming victims of violence, including murder. Politicians must continue to fight for disadvantaged groups, even if their stances do not gain votes.

The results of three elections in different parts of the world have been cast by pundits as proof that politicians who embrace "identity politics" risk being punished for it at the polls. In each case, this narrative has pointed to an emphasis on LGBT rights as being politically risky and somehow divisive.

Last year, in a plebiscite, a slight majority of the Colombian people rejected the negotiated peace agreement between the government and FARC (Revolutionary Armed Forces of Colombia) guerrillas. Some observers believed that many voters had treated the vote as a referendum on the government's overall performance—as tends to happen with many referendums. In that vein, some analysts attributed the loss to "gender politics."

The Constitutional Court had removed barriers to adopting children for gay individuals and couples in 2015 and legalized same-sex marriage in 2016. On top of that, months before the plebiscite the education minister, a lesbian, had proposed mixed bathrooms and changes to school uniforms to put less emphasis on gender. She also wanted to create a manual to curb discrimination based on sexual orientation in schools. Her proposals met fierce opposition from conservative politicians.

Opponents linked the issue with the peace process, in part, misusing the fact that the education minister had become one of the central spokespersons for the government's "yes" campaign on the peace agreement. The opposition falsely claimed that the peace agreement undermined family values and supported non-traditional views on gender and sexual orientation. The term "gay colonization" was coined.

Analyzing the unexpected electoral loss of Hillary Clinton in the US presidential elections in November, professor Mark Lilla argued in an op-ed in *The New York Times* that her campaign had "slipped" into the rhetoric of diversity, calling out explicitly to African-American, Latino, LGBT, and women voters while saying nothing of direct resonance to white working-class voters that have long been part of her party's base. In his telling, this led many white working class voters to feel abandoned.

He said that national politics is not about "difference" but about commonality, and that Clinton's campaign failed to speak clearly enough to issues like economic justice that cut across group lines. In a campaign that set out to embrace diversity, white, rural, religious Americans started to see themselves as a disadvantaged group whose identity and real-world needs were being ignored.

In the Netherlands, the March 15 election ended in a

dramatic loss for the Dutch Labor Party. Martin Sommer, a leading pundit, gave his analysis in the Dutch newspaper *Volkskrant*. According to him, the Dutch Labor Party had neglected to address issues of major concern for the general public, in favor of a narrow focus on specific interests of minority groups. He echoed Lilla's views. The Dutch education minister, a Labor Party member, had opened a gender-neutral bathroom in her ministry and gave interviews about why she thought it was important to introduce them. Sommer contended that transgender people whose interests would be served by this arrangement are only a very, very small percentage of the population and that by addressing this issue the minister had alienated the majority of voters.

Whatever one thinks of the term, public unhappiness with "identity politics" has shown itself to be a complicated and volatile political rallying cry. Many of the questions Lilla and others have written on are of course worth exploring. But it's dangerous and intellectually bankrupt to claim that the right lesson to draw from all of this is that politicians have gone too far in embracing diversity and standing up for the rights of women, racial minorities, LGBT people, or anyone else. Political leaders may well need to look for new ways to speak to the needs and interests of groups who feel alienated by mainstream politics, but they shouldn't embrace bigotry as a cheap and easy way to get there.

LGBT activists advocate for equal rights and nondiscrimination. They do not claim special or extra rights. They aspire to a society where LGBT people are not bullied at work or in school and have the same relationship rights as others do. Equality and nondiscrimination are values that concern everyone in society. They require a robust defense. Because the values of human rights depend foremost on the ability to empathize with others—to recognize the importance of treating others the way we would want to be treated—they are especially vulnerable when the argument of the majority versus minorities is invoked.

Politics that stops talking about minority rights on the theory that upholding them is "divisive" or makes it harder to win over majority voting blocs, will only lead to a more fragmented society, not bring people together. Instead political leaders should make clear that rights are not a zero-sum game—protecting my rights does not undermine yours. On the contrary, it creates a framework we can all rely on if our rights come under threat.

EVALUATING THE AUTHOR'S ARGUMENTS:

In this viewpoint, Boris Dittrich gives examples of politicians who may have lost elections due to their support of disadvantaged groups. Yet the author argues that politicians should embrace and support diversity, regardless of whether it hurts their election campaigns. What are the pros and cons of promoting one's ideals at the potential cost of losing an election?

Keep Identity Politics but Change the Message

Mala Kumar

"Identity politics allows us a lens into what is working where and for whom."

In the following viewpoint, Mala Kumar argues that identity politics can address poverty. As an example, the author notes how many white men have made money through tech companies, in part because they receive more financial funding. To improve economics for everyone, the country must understand what works for each group, she says. She then addresses the way identity politics are discussed and suggests that its messages should include and unite people of all races. Kumar is a writer and technology expert with a focus on using communication technologies to help marginalized people and communities.

AS YOU READ, CONSIDER THE FOLLOWING QUESTIONS:
1. How is gender equality connected to quality of living, according to the source cited in the article?
2. How does identity affect economic opportunities, according to the author?
3. What is the problem with the message of identity politics, according to the author?

Many conference rooms across America continue to be filled with white men. White men continue to amass greater wealth and power than those in any other group.

Assuming that the electoral college dooms us all on December 19th by confirming Donald Trump as President, who at last count had 2 million fewer votes than Hillary Clinton, there is going to be a long and bitter existential debate on the left. The current mode du jour is that liberal "identity politics" is what tanked the Electoral College count. While I don't deny the merit of that specific argument, it would be remiss of me to not call out one glaring issue with dropping identity politics from the discourse of leftist politics: Identity politics are a great way to address poverty.

If our ultimate path to winning an election is winning the economy, and if we have a moral obligation to ensure no one goes hungry or homeless, how poverty is addressed must be at the center of the political conversation. In 2015, four out of the ten countries with the highest quality of living also placed in the top ten in terms of gender equality. One of the countries with a top ten gender equality score—Rwanda—is one of Africa's fastest growing economies and has one of the highest quality of living in the continent. No s—t. Women are more than half the population of most countries, so of course empowering women to live safe, productive lives benefits everyone in the country. But in order to get to that point, something has to be done to address the root causes of the problem. In Rwanda's case, the "solution" was tragic—the country went through a genocide in which a massive portion of the male population was killed, so women were a large part of the reconstruction effort. Fortunately those attitudes of gender inclusion have largely prevailed, and women make up more than half of the Rwandan Parliament.

Other than genocide, how can we address the cultural barriers that prevent women, ethnic, racial, gender expression or other minorities from achieving economic prosperity, thereby lifting everyone in the country? Identity politics, plain and simple. If we as a society are scared to address the myriad of cultural factors that affect segments of our population, how can we expect to propose real solutions? Bringing jobs to the rust belt isn't enough if women, black people and Hispanics in the area are prevented from the same employment opportunities as white men. Identity politics allows us a lens into what is working where and for whom, and that lens is critical to advancing economic well being of the overall population of any country.

Identity politics also provides another valuable lens to economic health, one that Bernie Sanders has been shouting about for 40 years—income inequality. The overwhelming majority of economic growth in the past decade has gone to the top 1%, and the majority of that wealth has gone to white men. The ten wealthiest people in the country are all white men. With the exception of Warren Buffet and (arguably) the Koch brothers, all of them made their money in tech. The tech industry has boomed in the past decade, with venture capital (VC) funding doing the heavy lifting in early funding of companies like Uber and AirBNB. The breakdown of VC funding through the identity politics lens is telling: statistically speaking, black female-led tech companies raise 0% of all VC funding, despite a 300%+ increase in the number of black female-led companies since the 90s. Look at the numbers and try to make the argument that identity isn't hugely relevant to addressing economic growth in America. I dare you.

I will be the first to admit that we on the left cannot have it both ways. There are undoubtedly problems that disproportionately affect the white majority. If we want to continue to use identity politics as a way forward, we can't be afraid to address issues facing specifically the

FAST FACT

The top five countries with the smallest gender gap are Iceland, Finland, Norway, Sweden, and Rwanda. The United States is number 45.

white community, especially if the current demographic shift means they will go from the majority to the plurality in the next generation.

Moving beyond the merits of identity politics in economic well being is the issue of messaging. Messaging on "white issues" obviously must be handled respectfully for both white and non-white people, as there is rarely a single community in America in which white people do worse than PoCs, and given that America was largely built on the backs of black slaves. Despite the possibly explosive implications, we need to recognize that though "white culture" in America is loose and charged construct, it does have implications that need to be addressed.

The most common argument against identity politics I hear from the right is that they are "divisive" and "exclusionary." Divisive to whom? To white people, mostly. Until this point, the left has not done a great job of articulating the majority of any population doesn't need to be specifically addressed like the minority. For decades, if not centuries, minority needs barely made it to mainstream politics or media. Solutions were built for the majority and minorities were left to figure out how to make it work in their own lives. Arguably for the first time in American history, the needs of people outside the majority are featured. But in that amazing phenomenon, much of the majority felt like they were left out. Seeing that the new right is the alt-right is white supremacy, I'm going to take a wild stab and say it's thus up to the left to figure out how to properly message "majority inclusion." Again, I argue the solution is not to drop identity politics, no matter how tempting.

I could probably write a dissertation on this topic, but I'll leave my last point as something I have long been arguing—America needs to get better at embracing nuance. It is shameful that large swaths of our population find a cultural penchant to being uneducated and/or poorly informed and/or incapable of understanding details. America has been responsible for some of the greatest achievements in nearly every academic, professional and technological domain. We should not relish in not knowing things. We should collectively embrace that most things require some understanding of math, history, education, and overall context. We should collectively embrace that is our moral obligation to remain aware of who we are, where we are and how our actions affect others. It is the assault on intelligence that is our problem, not using identity politics to better understand our world.

We have a long way to go and, with Donald Trump in The White House, a lot of damage control to do. If and when we get a second to stop and breathe, I hope the political left continues to embrace higher thought, adopts better messaging and with that, one of the best tools we have in bettering America—identity politics.

EVALUATING THE AUTHOR'S ARGUMENTS:

Viewpoint author Mala Kumar suggests that identity politics have value, but their message needs to be reworded. How can a message affect people differently depending on its wording? Can you think of a message that would include people of all races in the quest for equality?

Facts About Intersectionality and Identity Politics

Editor's note: These facts can be used in reports to add credibility when making important points or claims.

- Identity politics refers to political views based on race, religion, social background, and similar factors. Identity politics can be used to draw people together based on those shared qualities. These groups are smaller than traditional political party groups. Critics of identity politics often claim it divides people. Advocates say that recognizing different identities gives voices to people who have been ignored.

- Intersectionality is a theory that addresses discrimination. It suggests that people may be affected by several disadvantages or forms of discrimination. These can include race, class, gender identity, sexual orientation, physical or mental conditions, religion, and other factors. Someone facing multiple forms of oppression will likely have different experiences than people facing only one form.

- The idea of intersectionality arose out of the experiences of African American women in the 1970s. They faced sexism in the feminist movement and racism in the civil rights movement. They began to call for a form of black feminism to combat the different forms of oppression faced by women of color.

- The term "intersectionality" was developed by Kimberlé Crenshaw, a law professor and social theorist. She used the term in a 1989 paper "Demarginalizing the Intersection of Race and Sex: A Black Feminist Critique of Antidiscrimination Doctrine, Feminist Theory and Antiracist Politics."

- In politics, a liberal party typically wants political reform and focuses on individual rights and freedoms. A conservative party typically holds to traditional values and attitudes and is cautious about change. Intersectionality and identity politics are most often associated with liberals. However, conservative values can also be a form of identity politics.

- According to Pew Research, in 2016, the median average wealth of all US households was $97,300. The median wealth of white households was $171,000. For Hispanic households it was $20,600. For African American households it was $17,100. The recession of 2007–2009 affected middle- and lower-income people of all races, with each group losing money. Only families in the upper income range prior to the recession gained wealth between 2007 and 2016.
- Class struggle is the conflict of interest between the workers and "ruling class." In America, the ruling class would be the people in charge of businesses and the government.

Organizations to Contact

The editors have compiled the following list of organizations concerned with the issues debated in this book. The descriptions are derived from materials provided by the organizations. All have publications or information available for interested readers. The list was compiled on the date of publication of the present volume; the information provided here may change. Be aware that many organizations take several weeks or longer to respond to inquiries, so allow as much time as possible for the receipt of requested materials.

The American Association of People with Disabilities (AAPD)

2013 H Street, NW, 5th Floor, Washington, DC 20006
(202) 521-4316; (800) 840-8844
website: https://www.aapd.com/
This group calls for solidarity among everyone who loves justice and equality. AAPD is a bridge between the disability community and the community at large. Its advocacy programs aim to improve the lives of people with disabilities and increase their political and economic power.

American Civil Liberties Union (ACLU)

125 Broad Street, 18th Floor, New York NY 10004
(212) 549-2500
contact page: https://www.aclu.org/general-feedback
website: www.aclu.org
The ACLU works "to defend and preserve the individual rights and liberties guaranteed by the Constitution and laws of the United States." The organization's website discusses many rights issues and links to online publications.

Amnesty International

Calle Luz Saviñon 519 Colonia del Valle, Benito Juarez 03100 Ciudad de Mexico, Mexico
+44-20-74135500
e-mail: contactus@amnesty.org
website: https://www.amnesty.org/en/
Amnesty International is an international nongovernmental organization focused on human rights. The organization's interests range from torture and the death penalty to free speech. More than 7 million people in over 150 countries and territories are members.

Echoing Ida

300 Frank H. Ogawa Plaza, Suite 700, Oakland, CA 94612
(510) 663-8300
website: echoingida.org
Echoing Ida's goal is to amplify Black women and nonbinary writers as experts in media. The website includes writings on a variety of subjects, such as Media & Culture, Health, and Sexuality.

International Labour Organization

4 route des Morillons, CH-1211, Genève 22, Switzerland
+41 (0) 22-799-6111
email: ilo@ilo.org
website: www.ilo.org/
The International Labour Organization is a United Nations agency. The ILO works with governments, employers, and workers representatives to promote decent work for all women and men. Representatives of 187 countries are involved in setting labor standards and developing policies and programs.

The National Alliance on Mental Illness (NAMI)

3803 N. Fairfax Drive, Suite 100, Arlington, VA 22203
(703) 524-7600
contact page: https://www.nami.org/Contact-Us
website: https://www.nami.org/
A grassroots mental health organization dedicated to building better lives for those affected by mental illness. The group offers educational

programs, a helpline, and public awareness events and activities. It also helps shape public policy relating to mental illness.

National Association for the Advancement of Colored People (NAACP)
4805 Mt. Hope Drive, Baltimore MD 21215
(877) NAACP-98
email: actso@naacpnet.org
website: http://www.naacp.org/
Founded in 1909, the NAACP's mission is "to ensure the political, educational, social, and economic equality of rights of all persons." Top issues include civic engagement, environment and climate justice, and health.

National Disability Rights Network
820 1st Street NE, Suite 740, Washington, DC 20002
(202) 408-9514
TTY: (220)408-9521
email: info@ndrn.org
website: http://www.ndrn.org/
A nonprofit organization dedicated to improving the lives of people with disabilities. The group advocates for laws protecting civil and human rights. Public policy addresses education, employment, health care, and more.

Voto Latino
PO Box 35608, Washington DC 20033
(202) 386-6374
email: info@votolatino.org
website: votolatino.org/
This nonpartisan organization empowers young Latino voters. "Voto Latino is dedicated to bringing new and diverse voices to develop leaders by engaging youth, media, technology and celebrities to promote positive change."

For Further Reading

Books

Bawer, Bruce. *The Victims' Revolution: The Rise of Identity Studies and the Closing of the Liberal Mind*. New York, NY: Broadside e-books, 2012. The author critiques identity-based college courses, claiming that they lead to poor thinking and political confusion.

Collins, Patricia Hill, and Sirma Bilge. *Intersectionality* (Key Concepts). Cambridge, UK: Polity, 2016. The authors provide an introduction to the field of intersectionality. They analyze its emergence and growth, plus some of the diverse topics it covers.

Crenshaw, Kimberlé. *On Intersectionality: Essential Writings*. New York, NY: New Press, 2019. A collection of writings by the scholar who first coined the term "intersectionality."

Davis, Angela Y. *Women, Race, & Class*. New York, NY: Vintage, 2011. A study of the women's liberation movement in America, focusing on problems of racism and classism in the movement.

Fukuyama, Francis. *Identity: The Demand for Dignity and the Politics of Resentment*. New York, NY: Farrar, Straus and Giroux, 2018. An examination of identity politics and what it means for affairs of state.

Grzanka, Patrick. *Intersectionality: A Foundations and Frontiers Reader*. Abingdon, UK: Routledge, 2014. A scholarly look at intersectionality studies. The book covers the origins and rationale of intersectionality, along with applications in policy and research.

Hancock, Ange-Marie. *Intersectionality: An Intellectual History*. Oxford, UK: Oxford University Press, 2016. This book focuses on the history of intersectionality.

Lilla, Mark. *The Once and Future Liberal: After Identity Politics*. New York, NY: HarperCollins Publishers, 2017. The author argues that American liberalism fell apart due to identity politics.

May, Vivian M. *Pursuing Intersectionality, Unsettling Dominant Imaginaries*. Abingdon, UK: Routledge, 2015. A scholarly look at intersectionality in history and today.

Romero, Mary. *Introducing Intersectionality* (Short Introductions). Cambridge, UK: Polity, 2017. The author provides examples of intersectionality to help readers understand how to apply the concept to life.

Periodicals and Internet Sources

"5 Reasons Why Intersectional Feminism Is so Important," *Rebelle Society*, August 7, 2017. http://www.rebellesociety.com/2017/08/07/kateharveston-intersectional-feminism/.

Barber, Kara, "The Basics of Intersectionality, What It Is and Why It's Important to Feminism," Odyssey Online, March 21, 2017. https://www.theodysseyonline.com/basics-intersectionality-important-feminism.

Bronk, Joshua, "The Fraught Identity Politics of LGBTQ Liberation," Brown Political Review, November 11, 2015. http://www.brownpoliticalreview.org/2015/11/the-fraught-identity-politics-of-lgbtq-liberation/.

Darer, Michael, "The Recent Spate of Anti-'Identity Politics' Hand-Wringing Is Proof That We Need Intersectionality More Than Ever," *Huffington Post*, December 16, 2016. https://www.huffingtonpost.com/entry/the-recent-spate-of-anti-identity-politics-hand-wringing_us_5851ea52e4b0865ab9d4e910.

Gaffney, Frankie, "Identity politics is utterly ineffective at anything other than dividing people," *Irish Times*, May 19, 2017. https://www.irishtimes.com/opinion/identity-politics-is-utterly-ineffective-at-anything-other-than-dividing-people-1.3087639.

Kirabo, Sincere, "Why Your Criticisms of Intersectionality and Identity Politics Sound Ridiculous," *Establishment*, September 9, 2017. https://theestablishment.co/heres-why-your-criticisms-of-intersectionality-and-identity-politics-sound-ridiculous-89b4116f9239.

Lopez, German, "The battle over identity politics, explained," August 17, 2017. https://www.vox.com/identities/2016/12/2/13718770/identity-politics.

Martin, Chloe, "The Women's Rights Movement Needs Intersectionality," *Verge Campus*, January, 2017. https://vergecampus.com/2017/01/womens-rights-movement-needs-intersectionality/.

Montanaro, Domenico, "Across the Divide, Identity Politics Unites the Base at Both CPAC and DNC," NPR, February 26, 2017. https://www.npr.org/2017/02/26/517366995/across-the-divide-identity-politics-unites-the-base-at-both-cpac-and-dnc.

Mukhopadhyay, Samhita, "While the Left Kept Debating Identity Politics, the Right Took Them and Ran," *Splinter*, October 24, 2017. https://splinternews.com/while-the-left-kept-debating-identity-politics-the-rig-1819799213.

Oluo, Ijeoma, "Thank God for Identity Politics," *Establishment*, January 5, 2017. https://theestablishment.co/thank-god-for-identity-politics-fba03f73be43.

Pluckrose, Helen, "The Problem with Intersectional Feminism," *Areo*, February 15, 2017. https://areomagazine.com/2017/02/15/the-problem-with-intersectional-feminism/.

Saroful, "How to survive in intersectional feminist spaces 101," Cross-Knit. https://crossknit.wordpress.com/2017/01/23/so-you-wanna-be-an-intersectional-feminist/.

Scalzi, John, "Straight White Male: The Lowest Difficulty Setting There Is," Whatever, May 15, 2012. https://whatever.scalzi.com/2012/05/15/straight-white-male-the-lowest-difficulty-setting-there-is/.

Scruton, Sir Roger, "How identity politics destroys freedom," Acton Institute, January 16, 2017. https://acton.org/publications/transatlantic/2017/01/16/how-identity-politics-destroys-freedom.

Smith, Mychal Denzel, "What Liberals Get Wrong About Identity Politics," *New Republic*, September 11, 2017. https://newrepublic.com/article/144739/liberals-get-wrong-identity-politics.

Starling, Lakin, "Here Are Some Ways to Help Build a More Intersectional Feminism," *Fader*, March 8, 2017. http://www.thefader.com/2017/03/08/womens-day-intersectional-feminism.

Uwujaren, Jarune, and Jamie Utt, "Why Our Feminism Must Be Intersectional (And 3 Ways to Practice It)," *Everyday Feminism*, January 11, 2015. https://everydayfeminism.com/2015/01/why-our-feminism-must-be-intersectional/https://denison.edu/academics/womens-gender-studies/feature/67969.

Websites

Center for American Progress (www.americanprogress.org)
The Center for American Progress is an independent, nonpartisan (not supporting a specific political party) policy institute. The website covers many political issues from a progressive viewpoint. These issues include education, immigration, LGBT, poverty, and more.

The Strong Families Network (forwardtogether.org/programs/strong-families-network/)
A home for over 200 organizations "committed to ensuring that all families have the rights, recognition and resources they need to thrive." Tools in English and Spanish discuss reproductive rights, gender-based violence, health care, immigrants and refugees, and more.

Togetherlist (togetherlist.com)
This site offers a comprehensive database of social justice organizations. To find an organization, use the search box or click on categories such as Women's Rights, Persons of Color, LGBT, Immigration, Disabled, or Muslim American. Resources include information on privacy, de-escalation strategies to prevent violence, and a list of unreliable news sources to avoid.

Index

Picture Credits

Cover William Perugini/Shutterstock.com; p. 10 Roschetzky Photography/Shutterstock.com; p. 12 John T Takai/Shutterstock.com; p. 19 Fun Way Illustration/Shutterstock.com; p. 25 Anadolu Agency/Getty Images; p. 32 Rawpixel.com/Shutterstock.com; p. 41 Mary Lynn Strand/Shutterstock.com; p. 45 John Lund/Blend Images/Getty Images; p. 48 ©iStockphoto.com/Aneese; p. 53 Hill Street Studios/Blend Images/Getty Images; p. 59 Pacific Press/LightRocket/Getty Images; p. 67 Roberto Machado Noa/LightRocket/Getty Images; p. 75 Monkey Business Images/Shutterstock.com; p. 80 Rodrick Beiler/Shutterstock.com; p. 82 Jessica Kourkounis/Getty Images; p. 89 Janine Wiedel Photolibrary/Alamy Stock Photo; p. 94 PH888/Shutterstock.com; p. 99 Rob Kim/WireImage/Getty Images; p. 104 ©iStockphoto.com/kasto80